I0202113

DEDICATION

In memory of Master Nan Huai-chin, and in the hope that his teachings and spirit will continue to shine through the many educational efforts at our school and the Great Learning Center.

DEDICATION

The Taihu School

A New Model of Education that Brings Culture and Values Back into Schools

Sami Kuo, Ph.D.
Bill Bodri

Copyright © 2013 Sami Kuo & William Bodri
Second Edition 2016

All rights reserved.

Top Shape Publishing LLC
1135 Terminal Way Suite 209
Reno, Nevada 89502

ISBN: 0615824722
ISBN-13: 978-0615824727

CONTENTS

PREFACE

The Taihu School is a new type of international school, which emphasizes Chinese and Western cultural values in its curriculum, that was founded by Sami Kuo in 2008. The boarding school is located in the countryside within the Taihu Great Learning Center located next to Taihu Lake in Wujiang, China near Suzhou. Together with Diana Hou, Sami started the school with just nineteen children whose parents were interested in having their children learn the best from the Eastern and Western civilizations, but particularly the deeper values of Chinese culture. It uses Chinese cultural treasures as the foundational thinking and values system to be passed onto children, and Western cultural treasures and thinking as the nutrition to help those seeds grow into a large tree. The growing student body, which comprises the elementary grades one through six, will soon number nearly four hundred pupils.

The Taihu School is popularly known throughout China as a "miracle school" because of the positive behavioral changes it has helped produce in children, and so this international boarding school has become tagged with its own "Harry Potter" magical reputation. Many of these beneficial results are due to the particular emphasis of its curriculum that incorporates the multi-dimensional cultivation teachings of Nan Huai-chin, with whom Sami studied for a great number of years. These teachings link the fields of Buddhism, Taoism, Confucianism, yoga, humanism, psychology, science and Chinese culture to produce a unified "human being science" of positive human development. Since few people know the actual methods and strategies used at the school or the deep principles and philosophies which guide it, Sami asked me one day to help make clear the "methods within the madness" for managing and teaching hundreds of children involved in all sorts of learning activities.

After many interviews, I have tried to organize many of her methods and philosophies into a coherent whole, adding mention of various corresponding Western educational ideas whenever relevant, and the result is the book you now have. It explains the higher educational purposes of the Taihu School, its various teaching methods, its overall educational model and philosophy, the correspondences to Western educational approaches, and its actual track record on influencing children along the lines of virtue and good behavior espoused within Chinese culture. If you sit down and talk to Sami, I am sure you will discover even more because the school is in a continual process of development as it tries to make many higher ideals work in practice. The story of the Taihu School is rich with Chinese philosophy and culture, historical and psychological insights, the teachings of ancient sages, and facts about the self-improvement principles of self-cultivation that we should all hold dear in life.

As you will learn, the school has many unique features that distinguish it from others, such as its emphasis on virtue and goodness, cultivation of respect and responsibility, life skills mastery, recitation of the Chinese Classics, martial arts rather than P.E., daily outdoor activities, Chinese medicine and agricultural education, a senior-junior classmates system, concentration practice, and various Chinese cultural values that are not emphasized within a typical Chinese curriculum.

The goal of the school, in accordance with many of Nan Huai-Chi's teachings, has been to teach the best from both Eastern and Western cultures in a grand unification, prepare the children to become useful contributors to society who can make their own way in the world through self-reliance, emphasize a foundation of mental introspection, virtue and good behavior as dependable character traits, provide the children with an understanding of self-learning and self-adjustment principles they can use throughout their lives, and to especially emphasize Chinese culture as the foundational values system in the curriculum. As you will soon see, the school has the goal of trying to produce an entirely new international school educational model that emphasizes virtue and goodness at its core, as well as the best from both Chinese and Western cultures.

Bill Bodri

1
THE PURPOSE OF EDUCATION

The best way to introduce the concept of our educational system and its principles is firstly to discuss some traditional ideas on the various purposes of education and the role it should play in society. As a Chinese school, our own ideas on schooling and the purpose of education overlap with many found in the West. However, they are also different in that we emphasize Chinese cultural values in our educational model because we see that much of Chinese philosophy can serve as a solution for some of the world's ills.

While we can cite many purposes for schooling and the educational system in general, the famous American educator John Gatto (author of *Dumbing Us Down: The Hidden Curriculum of Compulsory Schooling*) has often stated that there are three main objectives to educating children. These three objectives have been commonly taken as the three core purposes for education:

1. To produce "good, virtuous people" who have ethical, moral standards (an inner sense of right and wrong), good characters, who can get along with others in harmonious, cooperative human relationships, who are self-disciplined, who act out of principle, and who have a deep sense of their inner life and cherish values other than just materialism. This is the "spiritual purpose" of education, which is to teach individuals the difference between right and wrong, and instill within them a sense of goodness and the ideal of cultivating virtuous character traits.

2. To produce "good citizens" who truly love and care about the fate of their country, society and family and who are willing to strive for the public good and improve society through their personal civic contributions. This is the "public purpose" of education, which also includes teaching people how to live peacefully together in communities tolerant of the fact that other members may cherish different ideas, values and ways of being.

3. To train people to be able to take responsibility for themselves so that they can live in the world in an independent, self-reliant, self-directed way that is not a burden on the rest of society. This is the "private purpose" of education, or economic purpose, which is to help individuals find some particular talents or skills with which they can make a living. It is to train them so that they can be responsible for themselves and make their own independent way in the world standing on their own two feet.

Gatto often complained that a new and destructive fourth purpose for the educational system has slowly developed in the West, harming its cultural fabric and the roots of its prosperity. This fourth purpose now threatens Western society with decay because of its poisonous influence, for its presence has even weakened commitments to the three traditional purposes of schooling.

This fourth purpose is an unspoken goal of having the modern educational system primarily serve business interests rather than promote higher human values, and now demands uniformity and conformity. The hidden fourth educational goal of the modern educational system, which has developed out of its earliest Prussian roots, is to produce obedient, conformist, standardized individuals who will fill unthinking roles in industry or government, and serve the dual trends of consumerism and consumption that support economies.

These modern trends of consumerism and consumption that have grown over the last century are to some extent somewhat selfish and destructive in nature. While they have beneficially powered the growth of the world's present economic system, more and more individuals are recognizing that consumption-based economies, which must be fueled by increasing levels of consumer debt, produce many negative societal results and are unsustainable over the long run. Furthermore, the actual psychology necessary to support this type of economic system actually goes against deep cultural principles to decrease one's desires, be thrifty and save, be an independent thinker while cooperatively getting along with others, and try to unselfishly contribute to one's nation and society.

The life focus that has grown up in conjunction with this sort of economic system has become too materialistic in its orientation, too concerned about self-interest rather than group interests, too neglectful of conservation and the environment, and lacking many higher principles and ideals that ennoble life and fill it with meaning. The inherent emphasis within the debt-driven economies promoting consumerism is on personal greed rather than the ideal of improving human welfare and making an unselfish contribution to humanity. The resultant cultural thinking tends to increase immediate desires, personal selfishness and narcissism and encourages people to ask, "What can the world do for me?" rather than "What can I offer or contribute to the world?"

To serve this new fourth purpose, or simply because of a lack of careful thinking, many educational systems are now emphasizing various procedures and themes that "dumb down" students and harm the good parts of human nature. This new fourth purpose of the public education system can actually be identified as a root cause in the present decline of Western economies and culture because individuals are being trained to become the unthinking slaves of materialistic consumerism and are mistakenly taught that selfish values will bring them happiness.

No one wants these results for their children, and yet that is how the situation has evolved because many societies no longer emphasize humanistic values in their educational systems. In short, rather than producing virtuous, ethical, imaginative, adaptive, skillful, and independent thinkers who can find their own way in life and stand up to become the future entrepreneurs, innovators, leaders and heroes of society through all sorts of creative and beneficial avenues, more and more students are being turned into obedient, unthinking tools or cogs that can serve within a larger corporate machine. They often throw their ethics and higher ideals out the window when asked to serve its pursuit of profits, and then this corrupting behavior eventually becomes accepted within larger society, too.

The modern educational emphasis equips children less and less with the tools and thinking they need to gain control over their own lives, oppose injustice and stand up for ethical issues when it is right, make a creative and beneficial impact in the world, avoid or solve problems rather than create them, and find true peace, meaning and happiness in life. In stressing academia and the pursuit of college admission, it does a terrible job of preparing children to be able to find a life purpose or greater meaning to life through a path of contribution that exists outside of fulfilling limited corporate needs or government interests.

Right now, more and more children are simply being trained to unquestioningly fill positions in organizations which emphasize profits over higher human values, and which through wrongful action often harm the world, threaten its citizens and imperil its economic foundations. Thus it has become common for businesses to entirely ignore any ethical issues surrounding their behavior or any harm and suffering they may cause as a consequence of their actions, especially if those issues threaten the maximum level of profits potentially available in any situation. Their only consideration is now "higher profits."

While we need oxygen to live, we cannot say that the purpose of life is oxygen. While companies need profits to survive, we cannot truly say that profits should be their ultimate purpose. Thinking deeply, we should rightfully say that the true objective of a business should be some mission for society that is in turn rewarded with profits for its fulfillment, and which then enables it to continue fulfilling that functional objective. There is nothing wrong with profits, which are ethically achieved. Unfortunately, more and more firms are betraying this perspective of holding to a core mission and positive reason for being. Instead, they have replaced such concerns, and the normal standards of virtuous conduct such as honesty, with the desire to simply make more money regardless of the laws or consequences to society. This explains some of the present ills of the world that can only be corrected by a different educational emphasis.

If we delve into this problem, we can find that profits have become the purpose of corporations rather than the fulfillment of some functional mission that generates profits as a by-product, and in the pursuit of profits (rather than a higher mission) all sorts of immoral or illegal actions *are now sanctioned that our forebears would have rightfully rejected.* Those who object to this within those organizations are often attacked, criticized or even criminalized for trying to rightfully hold them to higher standards. Society, in turn, then deteriorates even more because we persecute or terrorize those who are doing their public duty and upholding the correct values, such as by reporting on corruption to stop it or trying to correct errors when they find them.

The elevation of profits above everything else in business, rather than the fulfillment of some ethical corporate mission or objective that in turn makes money, is one of the many reasons we have seen a deterioration in public ethics and behavior. Tracing the problem back to its roots, we can also attribute some of the fault to the fact that in our schools we have ceased stressing the virtuous ideals of being good people and good citizens. Schools now focus primarily on teaching academic subjects rather than proper conduct, and even worse, in the pursuit of raising test scores they have ceased teaching critical thinking, creativity and what is proper behavior for a human being. There is also a tendency to emphasize blind obedience to authority, which deepens the problem.

When the younger generation sees that companies can flagrantly break laws and simply pay fines as a cost of business, while employees avoid personal prosecution and are still well rewarded, it is being trained that being good people or good citizens is subordinate to the pursuit of corporate profitability. When it sees that a government can ignore personal rights and break the social contract with its own citizens at will, it also starts questioning the value of being a good citizen. Why do the adults running companies and governments act this way? Because society no longer holds individuals or their organizations accountable to the proper standards of correct human behavior, which is in turn due to poor educational policies that no longer stress virtue, ethics, good deeds and proper behavior.

The younger generation is being trained to just blindly go along with the way things are done, even if criminal or unethical, rather than object to or correct matters whenever they find things are errant. It is even being taught that it is not right to question or correct superiors when it sees something is clearly wrong or illegal, whether that be in the government or field of business. What type of world will this eventually produce?

To answer this you must consider what it has produced so far. A simple example is that the world financial system is presently in crisis due to what can only be described as a lack of ethics in banking circles and the government offices whose responsibility it is to oversee them. This lack of morality in pervasively defrauding others, and turning a blind eye to the negative consequences, must ultimately be traced back to the educational system and what we value as a society. To increase their profits, American banks initiated bad mortgages they would never hold themselves because they planned to sell them to other parties. Wall Street firms, knowing of their junk status, hid these facts and sold these toxic mortgages to clients while betting against them, while ratings agencies approved their fictitious quality rankings in order not to lose the chance to make money too. In short, the world financial system has been utterly crippled because executives and government officials permitted greed to be put ahead of both the law *and ethos of what is right and proper.* As we speak, an even greater destructive outcome potentially threatens humanity because profit-hungry companies without scruples are pushing the sales of genetically modified seeds and bee-killing pesticides, while ignoring the terrible health and environmental consequences that have frequently been reported. Once again, in order to support a corporate money-making process, many governments are failing to protect their citizens by looking the other way.

In Africa, the tribal chiefs had to seek concurrence of their opinions and were surrounded by thousands of individuals to prevent them from abusing their powers. In ancient Greece the Athenian youth recited an oath reminding them that it was their civic duty to correct leaders who ignored the law and public welfare, and thereby help prevent national decay. Today, however, such checks and balances have fallen by the wayside because people are attacked if they do their civic duty and oppose wayward leaders for their societies. We can only sigh when we read the Athenian Oath and recognize that its high ideals of civic responsibility and virtue are no longer held as important:

> I will never bring disgrace to my City by an act of dishonesty
> or cowardice. Both alone and with my comrades, I will fight
> for the ideals and sacred things of the City. I will revere and

obey the City's laws already established, and will do my best to incite a like reverence and respect in those above us who are prone to subvert those laws or set them aside. I will strive unceasingly to quicken the public's sense of civic duty. Thus, in all these ways, I will not leave my City in any way less, but greater, better and more beautiful than when I found it.

Unfortunately, these ideals of civic virtue, responsibility and duty have deteriorated in society even though promoting these ideals in youth is a crucial part of the purpose of education. It is no longer accepted that virtue, goodness and propriety should stand as the core standards for our behavior, or that businesses must act with benevolence, but instead it is now deemed that the idea of what is right can be shoved aside in the pursuit of what is merely profitable or efficient (or what one can legally get away with). The higher ideals of human behavior are now being increasingly neglected in the world, so we must start emphasizing virtue in our schools and in our real world conduct once again. It is wrong to just concentrate on turning out graduates suitable to blindly servicing the corporate machine and its amoralistic objectives of higher profits. The world is crying out for more innovation and creativity.

Children in these modern times must learn how to make their own way in the world, sometimes in locations far away from their families. Thus, they must be taught how to develop the skills of self-reliance, self-learning and self-improvement since they will often end up far away from those they now depend upon. In the larger picture, grades should not be as important as developing unique skills and talents that one can build upon to follow one's own personal interests in life and make one's own happy way in the world, generating a positive impact and contribution. Unfortunately, the educational objective of schooling has too often become a protracted process of university entrance rather than a means of encouraging individuals to develop these skills so that they can create a career along their life interests. You now go to school and try to get good grades so that you can go to college, graduate with the right undergraduate or graduate degree, and then get hired by a firm offering a large salary to help it become even more profitable. Far too often this has been accepted as the acclaimed path to "happiness and success" rather than the personal fulfillment of some higher life purpose. Not attending college is seen by many as a life error. I want to let you in on an open secret: you do not need a college degree to be happy or succeed in life, or even to become rich if that is what you most desire (many millionaires and successful people never even went to college). It is a travesty of our educational system that we make people think they need a degree or that it is always superior to diligent self-learning. Since "A" students often end up working for "C" students in life, parents must deeply rethink their ideas on what will bring happiness and success to their children from the educational system.

How different this is from the original American educational system that propelled the country to greatness, and whose results are symbolized by the multi-disciplined accomplishments of various notables such as Benjamin Franklin. This system produced *doers*, namely men and women of great accomplishments. The original American educational system incorporated religious training to teach morality, ethics and piety. It taught virtue and good manners. It taught the basic educational skills of reading, writing and arithmetic that everyone needed in life but most of all, it stressed problem solving, taking action, self-responsibility and self-reliance. It emphasized social bonds, altruism, ethics and life purpose. Several American founding fathers, including Franklin, Jefferson and Madison, even wrote about the importance of character education in maintaining the country and its independence, so character education lay at the core of the early American educational system and helped to make the country great. People did great deeds, and this did not depend on going to college.

In those times, because you had to make your own way in life without entitlements, you had to develop the character, mindset, relationships and skills that would enable you to make a living during all the ups and downs normally thrown at you by fate that test your survival. You had to become able to solve problems creatively on your own, and your output or contribution had to be something valuable to the rest of society.

Because nearly every family owned a Bible and went to church, the topic of virtuous behavior was the subject of many sermons, and thus was emphasized within families. People changed their behavior for the better because of this long sustained educational campaign and because of the *peer pressure* from others to adopt positive habits. Scientists have found that if just 10% of any given population holds to an unshakeable belief, that idea can then reach critical mass and spread throughout the entire population. It then has the possibility of becoming adopted by everyone, but it eventually dies out if the idea is shared by less than 10% of the nation. In addition to the education system, this group support system is therefore one of the ways by which the ideals of cultivating and upholding virtuous behavior can once again become prized and spread throughout a country.

America built itself upon these values of virtue and self-sufficiency that are now deemed unnecessary even though they are the basis of the entrepreneurship that built the country. In America, this heroic idea can be seen in part within Horatio Alger stories, which promoted a particular model of success that was absorbed by society. The basic idea was that an individual who lived an exemplary life, struggled valiantly against poverty, adversity, and misfortune while consistently working hard at improving himself could eventually achieve wealth, social standing, stability, honor and happiness. He could achieve this either by working on his own or for others.

This model, which helped America become a great nation, embodied many valuable ideals of self-cultivation such as the importance of hard work and strict adherence to virtuous ways despite adversity. *The Americanization of Edward Bok*, which championed the idea of a society driven by merit and that a person "got in this world about what he worked for," was another famous book along these lines, as was *The Autobiography of Benjamin Franklin*, which revealed a daily ledger system Franklin used for cultivating personal virtue and perfecting his behavior. Actually, Franklin's method for self-perfection was similar to the Chinese ledger of merits and demerits system invented by Liao-Fan Yuan in the Ming dynasty, and Liao-Fan's story on how to change your destiny has greatly enriched Chinese culture in a very positive way.

Since America became great along these lines, we must carefully examine this earlier educational philosophy that stressed positive character traits (such as honesty, thrift, perseverance and self-reliance) because in today's world we are not passing down to our children these values. Stable career paths are also disappearing, and workplace changes are now happening at a relentless pace. Therefore, because they must create their own livelihood instead of inherit ours, our children must be educated so that they are self-sufficient, not afraid of hard work, able to adapt to changes, and have the necessary positive character traits and skills that will enable them to create their own successful way in the world.

While everyone agrees with the three main goals of education that Gatto often cited, we subscribe to the teaching of Nan Huai-chin, our grand teacher and philosophical founder of our school, that there are two *fundamental goals* of an educational system that should be valued above everything else, and which therefore have received special attention at our school. Our commitment to these goals helps differentiate us from others.

The **first goal**, which is considered one of the traditional purposes of education, is that a school should help train people to become virtuous human beings. It should help train individuals to "be good people." Moral education, for instance, means helping individuals acquire enduring improvements in habits and dispositions that develop positive character. The goal is to lead them to more permanent habits of virtuous, responsible behavior that exhibit moral excellence, righteousness, benevolence and goodness. At the same time, moral upbringing means preventing dispositions, or helping to change dispositions, that are deemed non-virtuous, bad or harmful. Basically, you want to help people develop high standards in their moral development and personal integrity.

While most schools that take "producing good people" as an objective simply teach good behavior to children, our goal includes the extra step of helping children *transform the seeds of their bad behaviors*, such as lying, stealing or fighting. We have found that our own approach to fulfilling this objective, which we are always trying to improve, involves a much deeper level of transformative change than that which is produced by the traditional educational training methods typically used elsewhere.

For instance, we believe that we should actively help children transform their bad seeds of behavior into good behavioral tendencies, but don't believe we can entirely accomplish this simply by imposing disciplinary rules on their actions. This usually accomplishes nothing at all other than temporarily suppressing certain desires or behaviors, without creating any real transformation of their root causes. Because children are great at copying role models and absorbing their surrounding environmental influences, to produce a real level of transformation we use a variety of different strategies. In particular, we expose them to various positive "perfuming" influences we hope they absorb and routines that we hope will help them to adopt good behaviors and abandon errant tendencies. You must remember that education does not just come from the school, but also from the environmental influences we absorb from television, newspapers, the internet, video games, advertising, family, friends, neighbors and society. One cannot underestimate the power of these environmental *perfuming influences*, which is why we employ this strategy at our school.

In running a boarding school where the children actually live in residences on campus, we also have time to spend one-on-one time with children and try to discover the root of each child's behavioral problems. We then try to devise unique solutions for each child to help them achieve better habits while purifying bad traits. We don't believe in just helping children change bad behaviors to good ones. We believe that we should also help children polish all the virtuous predispositions they already have so that those unique positive seeds can proliferate, flourish and shine. When an individual has an abundance of good character traits, their predominance makes it easier to bear the faults that they may not yet have transformed.

There is no standard model of expectations for how we want each child to be because they are not standardized robots who should be the same as one another. We want each of them to shine brightly revealing their own individuality, but we especially want their virtuous personality traits and positive uniqueness to stand out. Our belief is that by strengthening their virtuous qualities when young and making them more secure, children will then be able to firmly depend upon these positive character traits later in life. If their foundation is strong, they will be less likely to stray into unethical behaviors.

People can definitely sense virtue in an individual's character; we all certainly want to hire such individuals or be associated with such individuals at some level in life, and so now one can argue that personal virtue is not highly valued. We therefore try, as a fundamental objective of education, to help the students truly become more honest, dependable, kind and considerate individuals who are respected by others because of their character and positive behaviors. The basic virtues, such as honesty, kindness, self-control, patience and integrity, certainly make life simpler and win their own rewards.

We have actually found, from the reports provided back to us by the parents of children who have graduated from our school, that our educational approach actually makes them into natural leaders at the new schools they go to and they exhibit behaviors that win them much respect. This is because our educational approach produces more confident, self-reliant individuals who can solve problems on their own. They have been taught how to bring skills and knowledge together, but they do so in a harmonious way while being kind, respectful and considerate of others.

Naturally, education isn't solely about teaching virtue, character and values, so of course we also focus on transmitting skills and information to students so that they develop the tools and knowledge they need for the world. It goes without saying that every school teaches knowledge and skills because this is required everywhere. The more important point is that we take Chinese cultural values as the foundation of our educational approach to teaching knowledge and skills. We believe that you must first help children set up their own internal value system *before* you strongly push skills training or require them to learn various types of knowledge, and we have selected Chinese cultural thinking as the basis of that value system.

Just as you have to first install an operating system in a computer before you can install other functional software, we think that the primary foundation of educating children should stress *Chinese culture and philosophy* while fostering the positive behavioral traits that will make them good people and good citizens. In our school we believe that knowledge and skills are just like a kind of software, and you cannot use them as a child's operating system. You must instill a particular type of thinking and select special values as the operating system for their way of thinking and doing things.

People typically think that Chinese culture is a body of knowledge, but actually *it is a way of thinking and life* rather than an independent topic to be studied in isolation. Chinese culture represents a wise way of doing things or looking at the world that has developed over thousands of years, and which stresses certain virtuous or wise behaviors. We take Chinese culture and its values of cultivating virtuous behaviors as the operating system we wish children to adopt as their basis. The way you perceive, think, plan and react to situations is a choice, and while we feel that the values system for our thoughts and behavior should include the best from both the East and West, we primarily emphasize the gems of Chinese culture that include the sagely advice from its many schools and traditions.

The **second goal** of education that we especially stress, due to Nan Huai-chin's teachings, is also unique to Chinese culture—coming from all three schools of Confucianism, Taoism, and Buddhism—is the idea that education includes teaching individuals how to find the inherent peace and purity of their own minds that is the essence of the real human being. This internal peace is the crux of human contentment and happiness. Chinese culture itself represents a wise way of doing and thinking about things, and since the essence of Chinese culture is cultivating inner peace, contentment, harmony, balance and quiet, we make this another core objective of our teaching method.

Lao Tzu says human beings need to return to the root of stillness, Buddhism teaches that we need to develop a quiet mind called "*samadhi*," and Confucius teaches that we need to find internal peace and stability in our lives. You cannot give mental peace to another person yet we are all looking for this special prize in life, so we try to provide children with the relevant tools so that they can begin to find this internal peace as an experience in their childhood. Once they touch it—and we have devised various ways they can find it—they will then be able to tap into that internal sense of peace and contentment for the rest of their lives. Once they touch it, it will not be a stranger that they are constantly seeking through frivolous activities.

With an understanding of what mental peace is as the foundation, and familiarity with how to cultivate it, children are then free to develop it later on in life if they choose to do so. We are constantly hearing from our parents and others that stresses in life are mounting because pressures are increasing and everything is happening (especially technological change) faster than ever before. Everyone nowadays is searching for internal peace and contentment amidst these turbulent times, but few people seem to know how to achieve it. We therefore try to give our children a few ways to tap into that inner peace and give them a basic understanding of how they can always attain it, but we don't overly focus on this ability. Nonetheless, we teach them the various life skills for how they can adjust their bodies and minds according to varying circumstances so that they can always achieve harmonious states of body and mind. This is because they will certainly need these basic skills throughout their lifetime, and yet few children ever learn these means for attaining mental, emotional and physical peace even though it is a strong objective within Chinese culture.

We shall speak in detail of both of these main educational goals because they help set our school apart from other Chinese international schools, boarding schools and regular schools. We are definitely trying to develop our own *unique educational model for a Chinese international school* that is different from the American and European models. Our educational model is certainly different from these other alternatives because of our objectives, how we do things, and because of the fact that it emphasizes Chinese culture and philosophy while drawing from the best of Western culture and civilization too. Our grand teacher, Nan Huai-chin, always emphasized that we should mix the best of Eastern and Western cultures, and we wholeheartedly try to do this at our school with the major focus, however, being on instilling deep Chinese cultural values.

The foundation of values espoused by traditional Chinese culture may truly be the only medicine that can solve many of the modern problems in the world, which is now being polluted by an overwhelming push toward desire-based consumption that doesn't produce peace or satisfaction in the lives of individuals. Chinese cultural values run deeper than the superficial consumption-based policies now propagated in the world to keep economies running, and are much more suitable to solving certain issues such as pollution, conservation, and taking care of individuals, to name a few.

For instance, while the present cultural mainstream of Western societies always pushes consumption, consumption, consumption, Lao Tzu (Laozi) and other Chinese sages talk about appropriately *limiting your desires* and whatever you consume. The focus is on saving, thriftiness, sharing, consideration and conservation. Confucius, as another example, talks about stopping any activity at the optimum point and not going too far. Basically, the deepest roots of Chinese culture teach us how to reduce excessive desires and *share*, rather than to be overly materialistic or selfish, such that we excessively consume and always demand more. These virtues, which are linked to the ideas of conservation, are the opposite of industrial consumerism and consumption, and can definitely serve as the basis of a more sustainable but growing social and economic system.

The original Greek educational system also talked about avoiding the hubris of extremes and cultivating a golden mean in all areas of life, but this idea of moderation and balance seems to have been lost along the recent decades of industrial modernization. While Chinese culture and philosophy emphasize saving and sharing, a common modern pattern of thinking is that people should consume rather than save, maximize what they can possibly get for themselves on an individual basis, and should calculate what is most profitable, efficient or legal rather than what is morally right or fair.

The important point is that most people typically think that the West is far more advanced than the East in terms of its educational philosophy, but as Gatto and other observers have pointed out, the Western educational system seems to have gone astray in various ways. The West has veered away from its highest principles in practice. Certainly the world has been dominated over the last one hundred years by the Western educational and economic models, but have they produced the good results we all desire in our hearts, or do we all sense that the results are somehow flawed and that the schooling process at their heart is now somehow inadequate?

As China grows stronger it will need to draw on the finest of its own cultural resources so that it does not get lost in repeating past mistakes or the mistakes of the West, and so while we highly respect the present Chinese and Western educational systems, we only want to *draw on the best from each system* to create something new. We want to match the best from the West with the best offerings from Chinese culture and its own particular values that stress proper behavior and the goodness of humanity, and thereby give children a new road they can follow.

In short, we feel that a new Chinese educational model should have purposes that run deeper than those now normally espoused elsewhere. A model Chinese educational system should focus on deep Chinese cultural values, philosophies and ways of thinking. It should especially emphasize various virtues such as self-cultivation, self-improvement, benevolent actions, harmonious relationships and good deeds. A school should also emphasize practical life skills other than just academic abilities in order to teach children self-reliance and self-responsibility, build character and prepare them for the real world. We have many things that differentiate our school model from others, and so I will try to describe various aspects of our approach in the next few chapters.

2
THE REAL PROCESS OF EDUCATION

All schools have the responsibility of teaching children both skills and knowledge, but as stated, we view skills and knowledge as the software you install on a computer *after* it already has an operating system. The question is, what should be the underlying operating system that will run that computer for good or bad?

We feel that this operating system should be based on the values of Chinese culture, which is why we have developed a Chinese educational model that is distinctly different than the schooling model found in America or Europe. As an international school we always try to introduce the children to the best from Western civilization, but our educational model stresses more Chinese cultural values than Western values, and Chinese ideals on how to face life.

Because we feel that a primary purpose of education is to help transform children's non-virtuous behavioral seeds and lead them to more virtuous ways, we have structured our school differently than most others to emphasize this goal as the objective. You can call what we are trying to achieve "education" or you can also call it "transformation." The idea is to teach what schools normally do, but to also help children correct any of their errant behavioral tendencies, which means to help them change bad behaviors to good ones during childhood when it is easiest to accomplish this task.

If a child tends to be lazy or procrastinate in getting things done, those habits will usually remain with them for life unless we help the child to transform them at a formative age. The only other option is that an individual tries to change his personality later in life *after* he grows up and awakens to the fact that he has a problem. This doesn't work as well as trying to help someone change his personality and habits during childhood.

Our approach is therefore to help children transform their behavioral tendencies along more virtuous avenues while they are still young. This has been one of the goals of the Chinese educational system for thousands of years, and one of our major means for doing this is by using a process which Buddhism calls "perfuming" or "smoking." We directly try to address children's individual behavioral problems, but we also try to invisibly influence the children by setting up a special surrounding environment that will slowly change the seeds, or roots of their behavior. This has similarities to Aristotle's idea that we teach through the multiple avenues of habit, by example, and by precept. In this case, we help to create positive habits that children adopt at the school, set good examples by the teachers we select as role models, and also teach the principles of proper behavior and good deeds through the stories and lessons within various Chinese classics.

Chinese culture has many works on the importance of virtuous behavior such as Chen Rong-men's *Five Varieties Of Family Traditions*, as well as *The Book Of Rewards And Punishment* or the *Treatise On Hidden Destiny* and *The Rules Of Virtue And Vice*. These books were all developed to offer guidelines for moral education while integrating Chinese Buddhist, Taoist and Confucian concepts. They deal with such matters as filial piety, good manners, propriety, virtuous living, good deeds, and recognizing the future consequences of one's actions. Perhaps the most famous of all is Liao-Fan Yuan's *Four Lessons*, from the Ming dynasty, which mixed Confucianism, Buddhism and Taoism to teach how to cultivate kindness and humility, reform one's behavior, and actually change one's destiny through the methodology of mental introspection (watching one's thoughts to change one's behavior) and merit-making (doing good deeds and practicing virtuous behavior). The Taoist work, *Lao Tzu's Treatise on the Response of the Tao* (*Tai Shang Ying Pian* by the Confucian scholar Li Ying-Chang), offered yet another simple approach to ethics and good deeds that covered thoughts, words and deeds.

Therefore it is nothing new that we should take upon ourselves this goal of assisting children in transforming their bad habits of behavior into good habits and more virtuous or kinder ways of doing things. This is the traditional Chinese way of approaching education, and therefore this is what we try to accomplish at our school. The problem with most schools is that they don't want to take on this task, but just teach academic subjects while measuring the progress of children through a grading system. Our grand teacher, Nan Huai-chin, has many times said that he has never seen this ordinary process of academic education transform individuals into better human beings. He always said that as people accumulate more knowledge, information and skills, without also attempting to cultivate themselves to become better human beings, they just make themselves more able to do greater evil, destructive or harmful deeds in life.

It is certainly not easy to help children change bad behavioral tendencies (such as anger, greed, selfishness, laziness, lying) to good ones. You cannot just outlaw or prohibit certain types of behavior and expect the seeds or root tendencies of those behaviors to magically change for the better. Therefore the task puts a very heavy responsibility on our shoulders that we share with our parents who also wish to help their children become the best they can possibly be for a fulfilling life.

Because we live with hundreds of children and thus see far more problems than ordinary parents would ever encounter in a lifetime, we have developed some definite skills along these lines. We always try to approach these situations individualistically rather than apply a cookie cutter approach to all the circumstances that arise. Every day brings something new when it comes to children and their various behavioral issues, so we are always learning new things and trying to refine our approaches.

Let me recount one example to help illustrate this idea. It is not a perfect example and actually is a bit trivial compared to the issues we normally handle, but will help illustrate the process we go through in trying to help children transform their behavior rather than just forbid something that's errant. Forbidding or prohibiting wrong behavior does nothing in terms of transforming the seeds or root causes of those behaviors. Nonetheless, genuine transformation should surely be what the process of education is truly about. Each culture, throughout time, has developed different ways to accomplish positive behavioral transformation, and while our approach is totally humanistic and non-religious, you can also say that it has a *spiritual flavor* to it.

For this story, you need to understand that at our boarding school the children eat their meals in set groups around circular tables. For each table of children, one representative child goes to the food line and brings back the meat for an entire table, and then all the children at the table partake of it. As soon as they finish that dish, the representative can go back to get more as long as the extra amount we always prepare has not already been eaten by others. The story I wish to relate is that one day a teacher noticed that a particular table was consuming far more meat than all the other tables, so he knew something was amiss.

This teacher's first thought was to tell the children, "You must be considerate of others when you get the food for your table. If you take too much meat back to the table, other tables won't have any." However, on second thought he quickly realized that this approach wouldn't work because it went against the natural tendencies of children at this age. If you just tell children to do or not do something, this type of admonition doesn't always work. To transform their behavior, you have to find out why they are doing certain things, and then try to influence them to follow a better course of action so that they naturally adopt it as a new behavior. If children absorb a positive influence, it can become the basis of a useful habit that they can use for the rest of their life.

Because our teaching method often involves a group suggestion system to find solutions to certain issues that arise, our teacher started to question the other teachers for ideas about how he might help change the children's behavior while going along with human nature rather than fighting against it, or just trying to outlaw the result. None of those approaches would transform the root of the problem and help the children at all.

Most schools or other institutions would normally approach this situation by coming up with some arbitrary disciplinary rule such as, "If you take an excessive amount of meat three more times, you won't be permitted to get it for one week." While this may seem to solve the problem immediately, it doesn't achieve our deeper goal of helping the children transform the seeds or roots of their behavior for the better. In this case, consuming too much meat instead of vegetables was actually bad for the children's health, so it was worthwhile to try to come up with a better solution in light of the long-term health benefits for the children that would arise from better habits. If we just instituted rules forbidding the children to satisfy their urge to consume lots of meat, the children involved would still want meat, so how could you help them transform their inclinations without going against human nature?

I often tell parents that **real education**, which is the process of truly educating children, should be compared to the process of slowly smoking meat to change its flavor or the process of perfuming clothing to change its scent. While sometimes the educational process takes place instantaneously at an unpredictable moment, as illustrated in various Zen stories, exposing the children to slow smoking or perfuming influences is a major process we normally rely upon. The idea is that you want to expose children to a certain positive environmental influence, and have them slowly absorb the influences of that special environment to their benefit.

This always works better than just imposing short-term disciplinary rules for children whose influences are soon forgotten. For instance, in Chinese cooking you can expose meat to smoke over a long period of time. As time progresses, the smoke will slowly permeate the meat so that it develops an entirely different flavor from that influence. If you expose clothes to the aroma of a special perfume, then after a while the clothes will absorb that fragrance and also become wonderfully scented. Since food or clothing only change their natural flavor or aroma very slowly, you should not expect that the influences you try to pass on to children can be absorbed in one day. The process of influencing children in this way takes time and commitment and a very positive environment.

This, however, is one of the keys to *real education*, which is to create a special environment of beneficial influences and expose the children so that they slowly absorb those positive influences and they think that this is the way things should naturally be done. Then the children, being natural sponges and mimics, will adopt those beneficial ways as a habit. We cannot always change their bad behaviors, despite our best efforts, but we can do our best to help them adopt wonderful new behaviors that help to overpower any non-virtuous qualities.

We are always experimenting to make things better at our school in using this type of teaching mechanism. We always try to design events, the curriculum and daily procedures in such a way as to create an environment filled with the very special positive influences we desire and that we hope will help bring out the best in the children's personality and behavior. We are always tinkering with these various things, so by no means do we claim that we have the answers as to what is best, and like everyone else we certainly struggle at times trying to determine what to do.

In any case, we feel that this is a much deeper educational approach than simply dumping certain subject lessons on children and expecting them to learn the topic, or imposing particular disciplinary rules to regulate them which, of course, are often necessary as well. You certainly cannot run a school of hundreds of children without certain disciplinary rules and regulations, especially when it comes to safety concerns.

The point is that, while the rules and regulations can prevent certain unwanted behaviors, they do not transform, purify or uplift the root impulses behind those behaviors, which is our ultimate goal. We are not just focused on mastering academia, but on this process of *positive transformation* to help the children to become better human beings. Even in the task of teaching various topics, we try to go more deeply into the subject matter rather than quickly jump from topic to topic. We want the children to be able to concentrate on the lessons and benefit from this lingering perfuming influence once again. In this way they can more deeply penetrate the subject matter, and learn how to concentrate for longer periods of time than other children, but we'll have to speak of this specific issue separately.

There is a deep philosophical basis to our goal of helping children transform themselves for the better that comes from the Chinese Buddhist theory of the mind and personality. There are many schools of philosophy in the world. For instance, some argue that people are born naturally good, some argue that people when born are like an empty tableau that can be filled with good or evil impulses, and some argue that people are inherently bad and must be trained to become good. Buddhist theory maintains that all individuals are actually born with a mixture of certain tendencies—good, bad and neutral—that comprises what is called the "volition *skandha*" of impulses and predispositions for each individual. These predispositions represent a mixture of virtuous, non-virtuous, and neutral behavioral tendencies.

Because each person has a unique volition *skandha* of predispositions connected with their self-identity, even identical twins will have very different characters and behaviors despite the fact that they share the same genes and are raised in the same environment. Your genes and the environment you grow up in definitely help explain why every individual is unique in the world, but they are not able to account for all the many diverse differences between individuals, or unusual things such as the fact that some children are prodigies in certain areas they have never studied. Some children exhibit exceptional natural talents for certain skills, such as playing music, which not even their parents or other ancestors possessed.

Chinese Buddhism and Taoism, like many other world religions, espouse the idea of past lives to explain the fact that certain skills you cultivated in previous lives can appear as exceptional natural talents in the present life. They also suggest that personality traits based on consciousness, such as certain positive or negative predispositions, will also be transmitted forward to future lives if they are not transformed during this one. This makes it doubly important to purify our errant patterns of behavior *now* while we have the self-awareness to do so, otherwise they will continue to pollute our character for many lives into the future and bring negative consequences along with them.

In Chinese thinking, this present life is just one of many lives to come. If you can transform errant tendencies *now* then the positive results will be wholesome fruits for many subsequent lives to come. Therefore the benefits from changing your behavior will not just be experienced in the present life but for the endless future, which is very long-term thinking. Learning more virtuous ways *now* creates a good outcome not just for the present, but also for the very long-term future of the individual and society. In this way, by starting this process in the vital formative years, we hope to help to cultivate well-rounded individuals who will be on the path to an auspicious future, not only helping themselves but in turn willing to help society to develop along the lines of positive human potential.

Whether or not the ideas of subsequent incarnations are true, the personality of individuals is definitely *not* entirely due to their genes or their environment, yet there is a degree of inherent tendencies that separate us from one another. Furthermore, there is a great benefit if our errant tendencies are corrected in this life because of the consequential blessings or good fortune this will produce while we live. Everyone wants to hire or work with individuals with good personalities and positive behavioral traits, and so the benefits of eliminating any faults in our characters early in life will certainly help us rise in the professional world or help us enjoy better interpersonal relationships, such as in marriage. Therefore one cannot say that emphasizing positive behavioral change is a trivial educational concern. Surely it must be a fundamental goal of the educational system.

We try to help children find their own inborn talents, intelligence and wisdom that doesn't come from genes, environmental or societal influences, and try to help them stand up with the good parts of their own unique personalities and skills. If children show unwholesome predispositions, we try to help these behavioral tendencies become purified through the right sorts of influences that we normally label "education." It is our responsibility, as educators, to provide those positive influences so that we can correct errant tendencies as quickly as possible in life and not unthinkingly produce individuals who won't think twice about hurting others or society for selfish gain.

Some of the tendencies that children already exhibit in life are "non-virtuous" (such as stealing), and if those tendencies and behaviors are not transformed at an early age, they can certainly become the roots of larger problems later in this life, which is why we should especially concentrate on helping transform their behaviors during childhood. Many people only start working on transforming their habits and personalities after they are already adults, but it is certainly best to get started at this practice of character cultivation earlier rather than later. For instance, if a nation is seen as being populated by unethical adult leaders, you must ask what is wrong with its earlier educational system that it has produced this result. We must remember that "For what the leaders are a rule, will the men below them be."

We do not just try to help children to change themselves at our school, but we have structured our educational program so that our children will learn various ways to adjust themselves and change their behaviors which they can continue to use throughout their lives if they decide to work in this direction. For instance, the children learn how to adjust their bodies and minds through exercise, diet, breathing methods, sound yoga and even meditation. You can adjust your thinking and emotions through various means, too, such as by listening to music or practicing calligraphy according to classical methods. We introduce children to all these various methods so that they become familiar skills that they can call upon throughout their lives, enabling them to continually adjust themselves whenever necessary. We especially try to familiarize them with the various self-cultivation teachings of Chinese culture, particularly Confucian mindfulness or introspection techniques (that can become the basis of self-inspection and self-correction habits in life), so that they become skills that they can always use rather than exceptional topics that they just academically study.

In terms of what Buddhism calls the "non-virtuous" behaviors of the volition *skandha*, we can say that some children have a stronger tendency towards anger, pride, arrogance, excessive desires or stupidity than others. Miserliness, haughtiness, laziness, forgetfulness, jealousy, resentment and irritation are also some of the negative habits and behavioral tendencies no one wants to see in their children, but which are connected to deep seed energies within consciousness. When we see children who are bullies, mean to others, greedy, dishonest, harmful to others, cruel, or cannot conduct themselves properly in polite society, the root cause is usually one of the many non-virtuous mental factors belonging to the volition *skandha*.

One can study Buddhist teachings on the various mental factors encompassed by the volition *skandha*, or the eighty-eight bonds and compulsions catalogued by the Consciousness-Only School, to gain a better understanding of the various good and bad psychological factors within the human psyche. Buddhist theory teaches that these mental factors must be transformed so that an individual can become more virtuous from mind-moment to mind-moment, and which actually stand in the way of attaining stable states of *samadhi* (quiet mental concentration). This Buddhist body of knowledge on virtuous, neutral and non-virtuous mental factors, as well as ten "omnipresent factors" of consciousness, entails a far deeper understanding of the nature of the mind than is currently reflected within Western psychology; its classical or Christian list of virtues worked out by

25

Socrates, Cicero, Thomas Aquinas and others. Even our previous idea of "perfuming" educational influences (if you expose clothes to a room filled with perfume the clothes will pick up the smell) ties into a very deep topic of consciousness that Buddhism calls the "transformation of the seeds of the *alaya* consciousness."

The ability to trust others, carefulness, a lack of greed, peacefulness, fairness, vigor and a lack of hatred are examples of character traits we all respect and admire in others and want to see in our children too. Honesty, compassion, kindness, sincerity, mercy, fairness, humility, patience, courage and strength are all positive qualities that have their seed roots in each child's volition *skandha*. We try to strengthen those good roots so that they predominate over any of the bad seeds each child brings with them into the world, especially when we make little headway in transforming their bad seeds for the better.

All individuals have a mixture of virtuous, non-virtuous or neutral behavioral tendencies and predispositions. One can investigate these various categories of behavior by studying Buddhist teachings on the volition *skandha* or the teachings on the eighty-eight mental bonds or delusive views that pollute ordinary consciousness. The implication of this body of knowledge is that we all have impulses, predispositions and behaviors we should try to transform during this lifetime, and others that we should try to strengthen.

Our grand teacher Nan Huai-chin often said that a primary goal of education should be to help uncover and polish a child's good behavioral seeds and tendencies so they shine all the brighter, and to help transform the bad ones so that they are no longer carried forward in life to become a problem for the individual or produce a burden on society. Parents and the school should both stand on the same side of this effort. This is a very high level undertaking that requires cooperation from the home as well as the work of our school and its teachers.

Most adults want to be very good parents and think that this means giving everything possible to their children. However, working at this objective of helping children transform bad behavioral seeds into good seeds, and encouraging more of their virtuous behavior, is really more important when we talk about being a good parent. This is the responsibility of helping children improve themselves for the benefit of their *total future*. Before you decide to have children, one of the responsibilities you must agree to take on is this task of helping them change their non-virtuous seeds of behavior into better tendencies, which they will carry forward into the future.

If you help someone transform bad personality tendencies into good ones, it is an incredibly great deed because it creates tremendous merit for that individual and society. Our teachers, committed to this task, are earning incredible merit from this undertaking. Their undertaking represents a higher purpose in life other than the ordinary pursuit of money found in most careers. The reason that behavioral change is so valuable is because that individual will experience a higher degree of happiness, peace and joy in this life without those errant behaviors, and greater society will not suffer the consequences of those errant impulses either. If there is such a thing as subsequent lives, or even rebirth in heaven, then changing bad behavioral tendencies now will also produce wonderful outcomes for that infinite future. If we don't work to transform those seeds, however, then they will continue to remain because they won't just magically disappear without definite cultivation effort.

Think about what the positive results would be, and how far they would extend into all the areas of his life, if you were to take a child prone to dishonesty and break that habit, teaching him to be honest! If one can prevent a child from smoking or taking drugs, one cannot even begin to measure the positive difference in outcomes one will have produced for their life. Often you cannot change bad seeds completely or cut them off, so whenever possible we take the approach of encouraging more good seeds to come up so that their preponderance will overwhelm any negative traits that are difficult to alter.

Even science has found that bad habits eventually become wired into the brain, waiting in dormancy for a chance to be used. We recognize this by trying to help children build new habits that will override those internal programs. We use our perfuming/smoking method to implant some better influences to surround stubborn seeds and slowly help to purify them. When a habit is very strong, Nan Huai-chin felt that it is only through a gradual, prolonged perfuming influence that we can gain some leverage and penetrate deeply into the psyche to loosen the strength of that habit within the individual.

We also teach the children direct ways to cultivate their minds so that they can develop mental purity, clarity, concentration and the ability to transcend the pull of negative tendencies and distracting influences. It is necessary to understand the great importance of the environmental influences. When schools are designed in a certain way they can produce the results you want, but if you do not carefully think about the influences you surround the children with, it will be harder to achieve any of your larger and more important educational objectives.

Now in the case of our excessive meat consumption dilemma, our teacher investigated matters further in order to discover some more information about the situation before coming up with a solution to the problem. This is another thing we do as a rule, which is to try to investigate any problem that arises at our school by understanding the background of the children involved, their personalities and family situations, their health conditions and other contributing factors. If a child tends to be lazy, for instance, we ask questions such as whether it is because they are sick, because of their bodily constitution, because of their classmates or teacher, because they aren't sleeping or eating well, or because of their parents' training.

You always have to investigate issues like this, which we can do because we are a boarding school. Living with the children, we strive to understand a situation deeply in order to come up with a solution to problems just as a family would try to do at home. Once again, in this way we are devoted to producing a much more profound outcome than the American, British, Swiss or European boarding school models that tend to concentrate primarily on academic results, and we can often come up with much better solutions than just disciplinary rules in order to really help the children deeply address their true issues. Other schools usually focus on disciplinary rules to keep things within bounds, and while we naturally do this as well, we try to figure out how to help children transform their innate behaviors so that they are less prone to disciplinary infractions in the first place. These are the errant impulses or seeds of behavior we are trying to help them transform.

In this case, our teacher discovered that the excessive meat consumption was actually due to just two children who were eating 80% of the meat that arrived at the table. The approach he then took was to tell the children that in order to get a second round of meat, they had to first finish all the vegetables at the table. Only then could a representative get up and go for seconds. This had the positive effect of influencing the children to eat more vegetables (as parents know, simply telling them to do so usually doesn't work), and consequently we noticed that the health of the two over-eaters even improved over time because of this new routine.

The point is that the approach to helping transform a child's unbalanced tendencies or inborn negative desires first requires some investigation to uncover the root cause of the problems. Only then can wise solutions for each individual and their circumstances be devised. Ordinary schools may not make the commitment to do this, or perhaps they just cannot spare the time, but this is one of our main objectives and the reason why we run a boarding school with such lofty goals. As our grand teacher Nan Huai-chin said, *this* is one of the purposes of real education, so we are committed to this goal no matter how hard it is. Putting our attention on these matters all the time, this is the best way we have found to help children transform their behavior. When the root causes of errant behavior are addressed and transformed, and when children are given the tools for cultivating themselves in a positive manner, this automatically trains children in self-discipline.

There are often many issues behind the fact that a child acts in a certain unusual way that needs some correction, and we always try to investigate matters and understand the situation completely before we come up with a solution to the problem. In dealing with hundreds of children on a daily basis, we have actually become pretty good at picking up on potential problems before they become bigger issues in life. We are not always perfect, but have learned how to devise some solutions to personality problems that parents with only one child and no prior parenting experience might find difficult to discover. We are not turning out standardized robots because we do not have a particular model of how we want every child to be. Our only goal is to help children transform any excessive character flaws or errant behaviors into something much better.

The idea of this story is to show that we take the task of leading children to more positive outcomes as one of the two primary goals of education, just as our grand teacher often emphasized. This is a daunting task not just because it requires a commitment of much time and patience, but also because the solution for each child often requires the wisdom of an individualistic approach to each situation. Once again, we want to influence our children to become better individuals and not simply manage them through discipline. We are interested in the process of positive transformation rather than just management. One wants to influence children to become disciplined by themselves by adopting discipline as a natural habit, otherwise the management way of imposing discipline on individuals will not produce a long lasting result. It will certainly produce an outcome you want in the short term, but not necessarily an outcome that sticks because it usually doesn't transform the roots of a problem. If you put a stone on top of weeds then you may dampen their growth for a while, but in time many will burst from underneath and simply grow up around it.

Our children's parents play a crucial role in the training task of transformation because this is a joint objective, and so they know they must align themselves with the school in these efforts. Many parents today believe that a school has all the responsibility of educating their children, so that when children err in their behavior then the school is wholly to blame. However, we believe that the parents also have a large responsibility in educating their children. Education is not just the school's responsibility, where parents can dump the children with the attitude, "Here, you take care of it," and then criticize how things are done if the outcome is not quite perfect. Thus parents must play an active role in supporting these efforts because the education of children is a joint responsibility and objective. Parents must recognize that we are their *partners* in trying to educate and produce better outcomes for their children, and so they select our school because they also believe in this joint goal and vision. We then work at this task together.

In Chinese culture, educating children has been a *family responsibility* for thousands of years. People must remember that the school is helping the family fulfill its own responsibilities for educating its children, and so the school is taking upon its shoulders part of the family's responsibility. This is why the parents must stay involved, and why you should select a school carefully to see if its principles coincide with what you hope your children will learn.

In short, the parents and the school must both stand on the same side when it comes to educating children and training them about values, proper behavior and becoming good people. Parents need to understand and support what the school is doing along these lines and be consistent in helping the school build the children's value system. They not only need to understand what the school is doing in this direction but need to match and reinforce its efforts at home to support those objectives.

To help achieve this alignment, we therefore require all parents of children at our school to attend a multi-day **Parents Training Program** so that they can learn what the school is doing on a daily basis, and so they can understand our values and various ways of doing things. They do not have to agree with everything we do or the way we do it (though there are always certain reasons why things are the way they are), but they must understand what we are doing and why.

The Parents Training Program is a mandatory 4-days and 3-nights event that all parents must attend once per year. During this training the parents learn various things such as how the school operates, what the children learn as life skills, and how together the school and family can work together in helping the children build their characters, learn values and skills and become better people. During the training, the parents also learn methods of self-cultivation for their own lives. Over the last few decades many parents in society have developed an adversarial attitude towards schools, and it requires a bit of retraining for parents to realize that they and the school actually stand together on the same side of the task of helping children learn life skills, academic skills, and becoming better human beings.

Many parents initially believe that since they are paying tuition for their children, the school's job is therefore to please and service them to do things the way they want. We disagree. Our primary purpose and responsibility is to help the children become better people using a system we have developed that we think is best. We are always trying to improve upon this system, and welcome suggestions from parents, but never veer from our basic fundamental goals and methods. If parents have a better system in mind, then they should pursue that way rather than enroll children in our school and try to change its objectives. Much of what we do is based upon Nan Huai-chin's *Confucian Dialogues*, and parents who read this book can discover our thoughts on the educational process and our views on the educational mission. This is the book you should read to understand more of our philosophy.

We have a certain set of principles and values we subscribe to and try to instill throughout our school, and we actually select children for our school by whether or not the parents agree with those values. If the parents do not agree with our values and methods, then it is common sense that they should turn to other schools that better fit their ideals, needs or expectations. When you buy a car, for instance, you can choose from many different brands and models, and what you ultimately buy should match your own particular needs and desires. You cannot turn a Honda into a Mercedes or a Toyota into a Rolls Royce, so in selecting a school for your children you must understand how it operates, the values it represents, the outcomes it typically achieves and what it is all about.

As an example, some parents might think that our school should teach piano lessons, and they might even volunteer to donate a piano so that this becomes possible. However, while we think piano lessons are nice, and while we certainly appreciate ideas from parents and often adopt them (since we are always trying to improve the school and our educational approach), in this instance we think piano lessons are not a primary need for a child's education. Playing the piano is a type of skill that children can learn, and in terms of computing technology, we are more interested in installing the right kind of operating system than installing many different types of software such as piano playing. Learning how to think, which includes how to exercise control over what and how you think when evaluating matters or how to draw meaning from experiences, is a need more primary than learning how to play the piano.

After much careful consideration, we have a strong opinion on what type of operating system and software is most valuable to a child in the long run, and that is what we concentrate on transmitting to the students at our school. Some parents are highly desirous that their children learn certain subjects that we do not teach, and in most cases those topics fall under the responsibilities of home training rather than school training. You cannot teach everything at a school because it would dilute your primary mission and main educational efforts too much, so this is something parents need to understand.

Nonetheless, there is an old saying, "There are no children you cannot teach, just parents you cannot change." We definitely always try to improve our school but remain loyal to our primary objectives, and we don't wish to weaken that commitment by losing our way in too many peripheral activities that parents sometimes hope for.

Most of our parents understand our primary objectives, and through our Parents Training Program actually experience many of the activities we teach at the school so that they understand our methodology and efforts. Sometimes we even open up this program to the public. In any case, the execution of our primary objectives, and the actual outcomes achieved, are the important things parents should consider when evaluating our school or any other. When selecting a school for their children, if parents don't believe in a particular system and its results, they should not enroll their children in that school but in some other educational institution that better matches their own perspective.

While most schools select applicants based on the children (or just accept anyone because of the money), our principle is actually to select admissions to the school based on the parents and the family as well. We select admissions by how closely the parents agree with our goals and concepts, otherwise there is no reason for their children to be with us. We do this because educating children is a joint process, and if parents don't want to work with us on this great task, it would be counterproductive for them to enroll their children with us.

Perhaps because respect for the educational system across the world has declined, it is a common problem in today's world that parents have come to think of schools in an adversarial "us-them" manner where the school stands on one side and parents are on the other side of the task of educating children. This is certainly the wrong perspective to adopt for a boarding school where parents entrust the total 24-hour care of their children to the school. We are not actually in an "us-them" situation because the parents and school form a single team of two complementary parts, like the white and yolk of an egg. Both sides must jointly work together to help educate the children. Because the school, of these two parties, is tasked with the primary job of education, parents especially need to learn how to support the school in its efforts.

If parents learn to have more trust in and respect for school, then together we can influence the children for even better outcomes. Instead of asking their children, "How are you doing in school? Are you being a good child at school and doing what you are told?" the parents are unthinkingly asking, "How is your teacher? Are they treating you well?" This type of questioning insinuates that the school is something to be criticized rather than the active partner of the parents. It puts the parents and children together on one side of the table, with the school on the other side, when its job is to assist the parents as their teammate and partner in educating the children.

The parent-school relationship is not supposed to be an adversarial one, but this type of questioning makes children the "inspectors" of the school, and because of this "policing" the children pick up the subtle idea that they should not necessarily respect the school. It is not that we want to avoid criticism or suggestions for improvement from the parents, or want to insist that we are always correct. The issue is that the way parents question their children can harm or help the school relationship, and when not skillful it makes it that much more difficult for the school to influence the children for the family's own benefit.

The way you talk to children is very important in influencing outcomes in their behavior. For instance, most parents don't realize that what they question children about, and how they ask questions, transmits their own personal values to those children. If you ask a child, "What did you work hard at today?" or "Who did you help today?", you are actually communicating to the child that it is important to work hard and help people in life. By skillfully changing the framing of a question, you can reward certain types of behaviors and therefore influence children to adopt those better behaviors. This type of skillful questioning is something that parents should practice with their children.

Praise has a strong influence this way, too. For instance, if you praise a child for being smart, they may develop the negative habit of avoiding risks and doing only easy things so that they always *look smart*. They may stop trying difficult activities so that they never make any mistakes or fail at any tasks because in that way they will always preserve their reputation for "being smart," which is what you have applauded. In other words, if you praise them for being smart, they will often choose to continue to "look smart" by avoiding the risk of being embarrassed with failures that might cause them to grow. Such things are indeed possible because of how you reward children with compliments. They will want to protect the "magical" status that you praise them for and this may slow down their learning.

If you praise children too much, they will also start believing they are great in that dimension and will stop pushing themselves to develop at the edge of their abilities where improvement usually happens. Natural talent doesn't forecast a lifetime of achievement in those directions. On the contrary, studies have found that it is often the humble, hardworking child, rather than the ultra-talented and mega-gifted, who, through deep determination and willpower, more often quietly develops his abilities to make something of himself in life. Through the perseverance of continuous improvement, a hardworking child can very often surpass those who are endowed with exceptional natural talents. It is the character trait of perseverance and persistence at continual improvement that we should teach. This is something even adults must come to understand.

In fact, those who are at first overlooked because their talents seem ordinary often develop into the real talents of society after they begin to consistently work on improving themselves, so *this diligence of self-cultivation is what you should teach children*. In other words, hard work can help you overtake those who have greater talent. The top performers in any area of life are often neglected and overlooked when they are young, and simply choose to persevere to develop their skills and talents to the utmost. The evolutionist Charles Darwin, for instance, was considered by his teachers to be slow and ordinary and Walt Disney was fired from a job because he was said to lack imagination. The world famous basketball player, Michael Jordan, was actually cut from his high school basketball team. Paul McCartney, of the Beatles, was never considered to have musical talent in high school. Albert Einstein, Thomas Edison, Winston Churchill and many others were considered men of little talent when they were young but developed themselves into men of renown. This is why we prize diligence, hard work, perseverance and self-improvement over natural talents.

If someone is a prodigy, you should basically understand that this is not a predictor of long-term success in any area of skill. This is something parents usually don't understand because they are fascinated by their child's apparent uniqueness that helps them stand out. Actually, it is perseverance along a course of continual practice and improvement that stretches one's boundaries and produces talent in any area.

We never assume that because some child has some extraordinary gifts that they will continue to be outstanding in the future, or that those particular skills will become the basis of their career. We therefore simply give children a chance to experience as many of their interests and gifts as possible at our school but don't *assume* that any of their exceptional skills will become the key to their career later in life, for how those skills will ultimately be used cannot be predicted. Thus we concentrate on developing the character traits of self-improvement rather than specific extraordinary skills. We can surely recognize a unique gift in a child but believe you should concentrate on moulding a well-rounded child, whereupon this gift will be able to flourish even more. By stressing the cultivation of well-rounded foundational skills, we help enable children to avoid eccentricities and develop all the necessary good character traits they will need for a fulfilling life, which may not always develop in the way which that gift alone might suggest.

As another example of correct praising, if you praise a child for making a good effort, he will absorb the idea that working hard is something valued in life. He will then tend to get very involved with problems and challenges, and not be afraid to try various solutions to difficult situations. By emphasizing *effort* you give children a variable they can control and work on developing, whereas by emphasizing natural skills or intelligence you are taking any results out of a child's sphere of control and providing no recipe for how they can develop themselves or should respond to failures.

In short, the way you talk to children, and what you praise or reward through your conversations, is something parents must come to understand has a great influence over their children's development. When you find a child doing something right and you praise it, this can have a gigantic influence on their behavior, and this is one of the ways by which you can instill in children a sense of virtue and accomplishment. Education often happens in a moment, and you have to be alert to catch those chances when you can help cement a positive virtue or habit using this type of strategy. For instance, you can form some ideas of the virtues you want your child to develop, figure out how to praise those characteristics if a relevant opportunity for the intended behavior ever arises, and then wait for the chance to speak the right words.

Along these lines, we feel that the modern Western educational system has taken the incorrect road of bolstering children's positive self-esteem through excessive praise and other methods that don't correct errors or deficiencies or prepare the children for the realities of the world. We prefer that children develop a sense of accomplishment from the fact that they definitely master their own life skills and become competent at handling some of the daily tasks of living. Of course we continually give them other projects throughout the course of a year whereby they develop a higher sense of confidence, accomplishment and self-esteem. However, we don't give them empty praise or praise them for ordinary things. We simply help them develop various moral virtues and life skills through repetition.

We believe this way is much better than the empty praise methodology currently in vogue, and we will see that the societal effects of "bolstering self-esteem" in countries such as America will not be as positive as their educators hope. In fact, the results from the current Western approach of over-emphasizing self-esteem may even be negative because if children grow up with no sense of reality or empowerment, they are being set up for failure in the real world. The world expects you to manage your emotions on your own and actually accomplish something before you feel good about yourself. This politically correct over-emphasis on self-esteem does not prepare children for the actual realities of the world, so policymakers for educational systems should consider approaching the issue of self-esteem another way, namely by emphasizing the actualities of skill-building that empowers children because they can see hands-on accomplishments. In our approach to teaching life skills, children become more courageous, competent and less helpless.

Along these lines of self-esteem and talking to children in an influential manner, over the years we have found that the best kids at school are the ones whose parents say, "Do your best at school and follow your teachers." The worst performing children have typically been the ones whose parents grill them, looking for school errors by asking questions like, "How is the school? Are the teachers treating you well?" Our boarding school is not a hotel meant to service children but to train them and educate them. When parents question children in a negative way, the children pick up on this mindset and become the center of a power struggle with the school, which is actually counterproductive for parents because it defeats their own purposes.

Once again our teacher's dinnertime meat dilemma can help illustrate this problem of parents misunderstanding situations because they don't ask the right questions, or ask their children questions in the proper way. Too often parents believe everything their young children say while failing to inquire deeply and ask them the right questions to get to the root of some matter. We have all fallen for this, even teachers and administrators at our school. For instance, when a teacher says, "Don't eat too much meat ... eat more vegetables first and then you can get more meat," a child might report this back to their parents by saying, "The school won't feed me any meat," or "The school doesn't want us to eat meat," or some other crazy sentence. None of those reports are true, but that's how children will often frame a situation.

Time and again very ordinary situations like this are twisted into absurd extremes by young children. Children especially tend to tell half-truths to their parents when they have been involved in some wrong-doing, and usually report those stories to their parents in a convoluted way (or not at all). That's the nature of young children, so it is to be expected. The unfortunate thing is that parents don't often realize this, or the fact that children can exaggerate or leave out missing story details that would radically change one's natural conclusions.

Children often fabricate stories for their parents, which is particularly common in the younger ages. Academic studies even show that parents have a hard time telling when their children are being dishonest, and find that the lies which children tell parents are most often an attempt to cover-up some sort of transgression. Therefore it is not unusual that we encounter all sorts of laughable situations where students do not report things correctly and parents become extremely upset because they believe one hundred percent of what they hear, but where the actual facts are so far removed from what was reported that it seems like we are watching a science fiction movie.

We have quite a few of these illuminating stories, enough to write several humorous books. We once had a student who told her parents that she was not allowed at the school to drink water at night. It turned out that she had a personal water bottle from home and had failed to connect the straw to the bottle correctly, but never asked for any help from anyone to do this. She came from a family where the parents and grandparents always did everything for her, and therefore always connected her straw, but because she never learned how to do this on her own, she never reported the situation to anyone and thus wasn't drinking any water at bedtime. Now, being weaned from this tendency for helplessness, she is one of the students particularly known for being able to solve most of her problems herself, so the school's approach has helped her greatly in becoming more independent, self-reliant and prepared for the real world.

To some degree, parents are spoiling children nowadays by trying to do everything for them, which is a harmful legacy of a one-child policy. We have even had some third graders enroll who could not even feed themselves. They said their chopsticks "were too heavy" because their parents were still feeding them at that advanced age, and so they weren't used to lifting them! One of our school's objectives, as reported, is to help all the children master self-reliance by learning basic life skills, so we teach them how to take care of themselves and break all sorts of bad habits like this as fast as possible.

Our school could not function if all the crazy things children tell parents were really true, but not knowing any better, parents often fall for their children's reports and never ask the right type of questions that would bring up clear explanations such as, "We can get as much meat as we want, but we must first also finish our vegetables." Children always say what they believe, and then tend to cut off the second half of the story that explains why things are the way they are. Parents need to learn to think for themselves that what they are hearing doesn't sound right. They need to ask "Why?" when they hear something that sounds unusual or unreasonable.

On our side, our teachers also have to be extremely careful of what they say, for what they say often influences children in unintended ways. For instance, a teacher might say that there are ten benefits to eating congee, and on hearing this some child may go overboard and want to eat congee, rather than rice, at every single meal thereafter. Then we have unknowingly created a problem we must remedy. Just as parents have to be careful of what they say and do, our teachers have to be extremely careful of what they say and do as well, even what they wear, since as role models they can influence the children in unanticipated ways.

Overall, you should know that our big target is to help all the children become more kind, generous, honest, trustworthy, optimistic, appreciative, respectful, dependable, disciplined, willing to work, responsible, well-rounded, polite and considerate. We basically want to help them correct their errant behaviors and become good, virtuous people. We all admire people with money, power or special skills in life, but when you think about it deeply, we all want to marry a partner who is really a good person at heart. We all want good, virtuous friends, too, and we want to be surrounded by good neighbors and colleagues. This is of fundamental importance since fortune in life is fleeting. We admire people we see who have virtuous qualities, so this is definitely of primary importance to life and one of the purposes of education. Nothing can make up for the lack of nobility of personal character.

Education should definitely teach children what it means to be a good person and how to act properly, and while this is often somewhat forsaken in today's schools, it is of key importance to life and human relationships. Therefore we put a priority on teaching these things at our school. We have specially designed our teaching method to train the children how to be good people, respect others, appreciate what they have and cultivate virtuous ways.

Of course, this does not mean that these are our only goals. We share all three of the main educational objectives that Gatto also mentioned for the West. The third of those educational purposes is to help children discover and develop their personal talents so they can use them in life. Talents and skills grow slowly, and so the most important thing is to help children get in touch with their capabilities and help them realize what they are capable of achieving. We try to provide them with a secure foundation for this discovery process, and we feel that this foundation doesn't just rest in academic mastery but in the principles of virtuous character development and other deep cultural concepts.

While some aspects of Chinese culture say that children bring with them into this life their own special skills because of past life developments, we don't really care about the reason that each child is different or why they may have some extraordinary natural skills and talents that they could turn into a profession. The fact is that everyone is unique and has their own special skill set that is entirely different from everyone else's, even different from those of their close brothers and sisters, and they can develop this to use it in life. While we try to foster the development of those specials skills and talents, or any special interests that the children may have, we never overemphasize them because at such a young age you never know whether they will play a major role in that child's life. We are, however, extremely interested that all children master basic life skills as well as academic skills that are the basis for self-reliance.

Once again, you never know how any of an individual's special interests or abilities will play a later role in their life, if at all. For instance, Steve Jobs, who dropped out of college, once took a calligraphy course that he thought was totally useless at the time, but just interesting. He later said that this "useless" course was the single most important reason that he was able to develop the elegant uniqueness of Apple computers with their multiple typefaces and beautiful fonts. Job's study of calligraphy, which he integrated into the Apple computers, certainly has helped make the business world a more aesthetically pleasing place, but no one would have ever predicted that this result would arise because of a "useless" passing interest in calligraphy. Therefore we are particularly keen never to kill children's particular interest or fascination with a topic even if we cannot help develop it. We especially try never to kill their imagination.

Sometimes children show a very great interest in developing a particular skill, which parents rightfully support so that it might flourish, but that interest never develops into anything significant at all in later life. The love of music is one such instance along these lines. Hence you never know what the interests of children will lead to later in their lives, and whether they will play a small or big role in impacting the world. The important thing is to try to introduce children to various undiscovered skills through your school activities so that they then know they have them. Those skills do not always come in the form of academic mastery.

Because "intelligence" is diverse and appears as many different forms of excellence rather than just academic ability, we can certainly say that different children are intelligent in different ways. Children may have many different talents other than the singular skill of academic mastery that we normally prize in schools, which is the normal measure of a "superior" student. Some children, for instance, are particularly great at using their body and so they are good at sports, dancing or athletics. In education this is called "body-kinesthetic intelligence," which is different from academic skills. This phrase means that a child has exceptional athletic or movement skills, and when we see this we try to encourage those children to build on their strengths through martial arts, yoga and other avenues if they enjoy those activities.

Once again, however, I must remind parents that even if a child is a prodigy in this area, no one can predict that they will have a future career in sports despite their richness of athletic ability or love of sports, and so we try not to overemphasize "giftedness" in this or any other area. Education is meant to prepare us for a future we cannot predict. We therefore simply concentrate on teaching children the foundation of virtuous traits and skills that they will need for life no matter what their eventual calling because one absolutely cannot foresee that future career or occupation. We have to prepare children for life without knowing the final outcome, and so we don't necessarily concentrate on particular skill sets that parents may want emphasized. We just hope that children can discover some of their unknown talents that usually remain undiscovered in a normal school system.

We also try to teach children *how to become self-reliant* so they need not depend on others but can find their own way in life, no matter what it ends up bringing them in terms of the ups and downs of fate. That is the most important thing because education must prepare you for the task of *navigating life* and engaging with the real world. Too often it is the parents who become obsessed with a particular dream that their child should excel in some special skill that may never turn into a career or calling. Nan Huai-chin often warned that parents must be very careful not to override all of their children's own desires and preferences with their own dreams, or push them to overachieve within a course that the parents have personally selected. You must allow them to discover their own interests in life and encourage them to find a self-reliant career along those lines.

Some children aren't so good at athletics but are good at music or artistic endeavors such as drawing, so we support the development of these skills whenever possible but once again we don't overemphasize them. How many of us were taught piano or violin when we were young but did nothing with it later in life? As a parent you can emphasize such skills but we dare not take on that task of emphasis at a young age. Some children are great at social abilities such as getting along with others, understanding other people, reading the social situation, and managing situations. Some are good at mathematics or literature because they have well developed "logical-mathematical" or "linguistic intelligence" skills. The special talents and interests children have are too numerous to list. We want them to become familiar with all of their skills, and hope that later in life they may choose to develop what most interests them.

Children have all sorts of multiple intelligences and skills at different levels of proficiency, such as "mechanical" or "emotional" intelligence, and we simply try to help them explore those particular skill sets so they know that they are available for life. Whether they end up relying upon them in a career because their capabilities in those directions are so great, or whether they just enjoy them during the golden age of childhood, we don't over-emphasize anyone's particular talents or call them "great." As I previously explained, doing so can be destructive.

We also try to expose the children to many different situations and opportunities so that they can learn how to be creative rather than just non-innovative copycats, which is a particular problem in traditional Chinese educational training. Whatever their karmic inheritance in terms of personality traits, skills and interests, we try to make it possible for the children to be able to explore many different fields of activity through a process of exposure.

As often stated, one of our main educational objectives is that we want children to be able to stand up and survive in the world on their own. At our school we therefore try to teach life skills alongside academics, and self-responsibility and self-reliance through the ability to overcome challenges.

If children learn how to be self-reliant, it is easier for them later in life to manage others, run companies, and influence both society and the country on a broader scale and for the better. Therefore we use a variety of methods to accomplish this special objective, and it is through these methods that we handle the problem of self-esteem that the West has blown out of proportion.

To train children in self-reliance, we teach them life skills such as how to do their own laundry, clean their rooms, and complete other ordinary household chores. Tremendous positive results come from the daily routine we follow that teaches the children such ordinary but useful skills such as how to wash and fold their clothes, how to clean their rooms, how to wear the right clothes for the weather, how to exercise properly and so on. We don't just teach the children how to do things properly, but teach them to live in the moment with awareness and do everything with a joyful heart without complaints or worries or anxieties.

Students who are taught to do these things develop confidence in their own abilities to do things. They can say to themselves with confidence, "I can do my own laundry, cooking, cleaning, ... what do I need to fear?" In everything they do they tend to develop an air of confidence, and because we don't often give tests but emphasize learning experiences and the development of concentration, they don't develop the normal test anxiety or fear of failure that children in regular schools ordinarily experience. However, you shouldn't hold us to this policy of very few tests since we are always tinkering with our system in order to try to produce better academic and disciplinary results. Nonetheless, we are more interested about the people our students will become and what they can actually do rather than the scores on tests they take.

When the parents of our sixth grade graduates report back to us on how they are doing at their new schools, they commonly tell us that they have become natural leaders in those new locations and their teachers' best helpers. The parents report that this has happened because their children have developed many different skillsets and problem solving abilities that the other children lack, and they are not afraid to try to do new things. Because of their confidence and abilities, their new friends end up relying on them, too, and they usually become the center of their group. Their leadership skills come from the fact they were taught to do everything themselves and trained how to solve problems, and so they often become natural leaders amongst their peers.

We also try to encourage the students to develop their own independent minds rather than just accept the viewpoints of others. We try to teach them how to concentrate so that they are not so easily distracted by outside influences, and encourage them to use their own problem solving and reasoning abilities. It is important that children learn how to think through situations for themselves, such as the eventual consequences of their actions, and learn to use the skills of creative inquiry and logic that keep them grounded in reality. The idea that an expert is the only one capable or qualified to come up with answers to situations is ludicrous, as history clearly shows, and is not something we support in our curriculum.

One of the special things we do at our school is *give them a place of calm and quiet away from all sorts of negative outside influences.* There are many reasons we do this, one of which is to help them become aware of the internal peace that is already available in their minds. We try to keep them away from becoming overly polluted by television, the internet, computer games, excessive cellphone usage and so on. We try to give them a period of purity away from all this – which is filled with all sorts of *real life* activities — so that they can establish a quiet mental foundation that is free of all sorts of pollution. We understand that technology can engage their imagination and provide highly customized forms of teaching, but we do not rely on internet technologies when teaching the elementary grades.

It is a terribly sad thing to mention, but it is also a real fact of life that very young children nowadays are also becoming overly exposed to sexuality by the advertising industry, television and the internet. Modern media readily provides all sorts of pollution and urges us to buy all sorts of things that are not good for either ourselves or the environment. Today children can now access internet pornography quite easily, and the more they are exposed to depravities they cannot resist viewing due to youthful curiosity, the more they will get polluted and drawn into an unstoppable march to a moral wasteland. Our approach to forbidding most computer devices on campus has the added benefit of helping to insulate children from much of this.

While some educators feel that there should be more and more computers in the classroom, we don't feel that elementary grade children should be stimulated all the time by computers and the internet, and have found that this actually has a negative impact on their attention spans, ability to concentrate, and desire to explore the real world of grass, trees and nature. Thus we particularly try to give young children time outdoors where they can experience the awe of nature and discover peacefulness in their minds away from the artificial world of technology. This is a remedy for children whose nervous systems are unprepared to learn because they have been exposed to huge doses of mental busyness and meandering, including images of violence, due to constant media exposure.

As they get older, it is likely that young children will eventually become absorbed in television and the internet and become affected by these influences, but at the elementary ages we try to preserve their mental peace and protect it from those influences as much as possible. At home on the weekends the children are free to explore those worlds as much as they (or their parents) like, but not in the school environment. In thousands of years of human history, we have never experienced a time where so many distractions were bombarding us at once and unsettling our minds. This trend is definitely making children's minds much too scattered, restless and busy, and because of this they cannot learn how to calm down or concentrate.

Basically, at the Taihu School we try to give the children a "smooth period" in their lives, which is what the golden time of childhood should be like, so that they can forever after remember what it is like to experience mental calmness and purity. After experiencing this mental calmness and purity and learning how to reproduce it, they will always be able to get back to this internal peace later in life if they want it. Even our parents learn how to tap into this peace when they visit us for training programs and learn how to meditate. We therefore think that *exposing people to the inherent purity of their minds* is one of the fundamental purposes of education.

We therefore want each child to be able to get in touch with the inherent purity of their mind, which is its natural characteristic, and realize that this is the actual source of human peace and contentment. Many creative or inventive ideas come from this experience of calming down rather than remaining scatter-brained, lost in wandering thoughts. Without experiencing mental stillness you cannot think properly, so it is important that we teach children how to cultivate this in their lives.

When children grow up, we hope that they will never forget this calmness and purity of their mind. If they can remember it because they once had it, they can learn how to get it back again whenever they become troubled or stressed because of life's pressures. It is one of our two main objectives in education that we should introduce children to their own inherent mental calmness and purity, and we especially try to do this through the exposure to nature.

The ability to be quiet and calm in your mind is not just the basis of the individual, but it is also the basis of proper decision making and great achievements in life. As Chinese culture teaches, *calmness is actually the root of the human being; the root is quietness.* Basically, children need to grow up in a state of more purity than is found in the world of distracting technology, and we try to provide that experience for their benefit at our school. We know children are forming fond memories of their experiences along these lines, such as just sitting on the grass and looking at an endless sky, and it definitely helps to shape their character and their ability to concentrate or be creative.

Let us illustrate this through a simple example that you might recognize. When you were young you probably ate your mother's cooking, which today you might still fondly remember. As you get older you will eat all sorts of delicious foods of various types. However, you will probably still always miss the taste of your mother's cooking, which came at a time when you grew up within a relatively calm and peaceful environment. We are trying to make such an experience of peacefulness available to our students so that they can always remember it because we want them to have that foundation for the rest of their lives. It is important that every student should have the experience of mental calm and quiet in childhood.

We additionally teach the children how to harmonize their spirits, bodies and minds through all sorts of adjustments they can make so that they can find peace and calm whenever they need it. During the day we fill their time with all sorts of learning activities that will help them shape their character to become better human beings, and also try to teach them the skills for success in life. But in teaching them various skills or subject matters, we try to give them the amount of time they need to go slowly and deeply into various topics so that they can master them. The availability of the internet today with instant answers makes it easy for children to become faster at whatever they research, but their level of understanding is also now more superficial. We don't force them to quickly flit from one thing to the next so that they never really master a topic, but try to stay longer with a topic until understanding develops within their consciousness.

The benefit of this approach is that because they are taught to experience inner peace and calm, our children can also easily learn how to concentrate. If their minds are always kept too busy because of constant stimulation, as you will find with most children nowadays, they cannot learn how to concentrate for long periods of time at all. In order to accomplish great things in the world you definitely need to be able to concentrate on tasks for long periods of time, so this is the skill we try to develop. We try to teach concentration in the way that we structure our lesson plans and by the fact that our classes usually last 90 minutes rather than the 40 minutes most schools use. Modern schools believe that children have about a 40-minute attention span (15-20 minutes for younger children) but we feel this is because they are just following the children's tendencies rather than training them to be able to concentrate for longer periods of time.

During the past few decades, the educational system has started training people for shorter attention spans, and you can see that people everywhere are now more easily losing their patience. Children have no patience today largely because they have been trained to be like this. A typical school might, as an example, offer eight classes per day with 40-minute sessions per class, and then think that this is great because it gives the children more choices of subject. However, in a 40-minute class there is really very little time to teach anything, and the students are racing off to the next subject before they really get deeply into the one they just arrived at. This is why we currently use a 90-minute class with four classes per day, although we are experimenting with 75-minute sessions, and we also run our school on a 12-days on, 2-days off cycle.

We previously tried a 5-days on, 2-days (weekend) off teaching schedule but found that the children would often come back sick from their weekend home visits because they would eat all sorts of sugary foods and break all sorts of balanced living schedules, so we shifted to the 12-days on, 2-days off schedule to try to create as stable an environment as possible. This regularity also helps to establish a type of calmness at our school because the children follow a stable schedule for a longer period of time.

We found this 2-week schedule works much better than a 5-day teaching schedule, and the children don't feel any loss at all by having school on a Saturday and Sunday since any typical day is filled with all sorts of activities all day long and they are spending time with their friends. In today's world, it actually seems as if the holidays are killing people. In ancient times, when science and commerce were not very developed, Sunday was a day for rest and reflection but now it's a day for running around frantically to eat and shop by breaking your regular living schedule. Along these lines, we have actually found that it actually isn't good for the children to have too many holidays.

What most visitors to our school don't realize is that the entire curriculum and teaching schedule at our school is based on the philosophy of creating an environment where children can learn things in a better way *because they can calm down*. We design everything in our school based on the principle of promoting calmness even though you can see children running around from here to there and involved in all sorts of energetic activities. In education you must go back to the original human being and tap into quietness. That's when wisdom can come out and when education can really happen, so we try to design that ability to concentrate or reach quietness into many activities at our school.

Of course we certainly also teach knowledge and skills at our school, but we make a special practice of focusing on teaching children how to polish their minds through concentration and virtuous behavior, since it is the mind that ultimately makes use of those skills and knowledge. By first polishing their mind and wiping away the dusts of distraction, the children can more easily learn how to master academic subjects and skills or even the mind-body connection we try to teach through martial arts classes. Nevertheless, we want to teach the children how to use their minds because the mind is the ultimate host, user or doer, and that's the thing they have to work on developing in life.

It is useless to collect skills and knowledge if the underlying equipment that uses them is faulty, and so we concentrate on teaching the children how to harmonize their mind equipment so that it can reach a state of inner stillness, quiet and peacefulness. In terms of consciousness, it is only within calmness that you can really touch your true mind and learn to think deeply so as to be able to make the right decisions. Kuan Tzu (Guanzi), whose methods Nan Huai-chin suggested may be the most appropriate for Westerners to study in these modern times, taught that you can use this way of calmness and deep consideration to solve problems. Buddhism also says that if you are able to fix your mind on one thing, there is nothing you will not be able to accomplish.

Mental purity, which you can achieve through moral improvement and virtuous conduct, definitely leads to calmness, concentration power and penetrating insight. When there is a strong groundwork of moral purity and virtue, the great blessings of a human life will arise naturally. Furthermore, it is really only in quiet and calm that you can enjoy life because you cannot truly know joy, for instance, unless there is a background of calmness within which it appears. These are just some of the reasons why we want children to learn how to touch the inherent purity of their minds, and why we focus on this as one of the educational objectives of our school.

To put this another way, in music, periods absent of sound are just as important as periods filled with sound because it is these moments of no-sound which give context and definition to the moments of sound. Sound is only decipherable because it appears within a backdrop of silence. Likewise, in a child, the moments of pure, calm awareness that we help them to cultivate enable them to retain a backdrop of clarity at all times. A calmer mind in turn helps them to define their actions better along the lines that are more beneficial, wholesome and fulfilling both for themselves and for those around them. When an individual cultivates this calmness as their inherent base-state, they will create the ability to make better decisions not only for themselves but also for the greater benefit of all, extending to their families and society a positive influence of improvement.

But don't make the mistake from reading this of thinking that we have junior Zen monks or many clones of the wise Master Yoda from Star Wars running around. Our children are just as rambunctious, energetic and even naughty as other children their age. However, they seem to know how to more easily reach inner states of calm and concentration and seem to be more free of mental pollution, which impacts their energy and spirit in a positive way. This is one of the experiences we are trying to give them in their childhood.

3
TEACHING EXTERNAL AND INTERNAL VIRTUE: RESPECT AND INNER QUIET

Although we have talked of our two major goals of teaching the children to become virtuous individuals and find the inner peace of their minds, parents and other educators often ask us for more specifics on how we try to do this. Therefore I want to offer some brief explanations.

When one wants to teach a child how to be a good person, we have found that one of the best ways is to **emphasize respect** both for activities and for other people. The Chinese people, as a cultural tendency, tend to show politeness to others, and we normally regard this as indicating respect. However, there is a distinct tendency for us to be courteous and polite with people we know, but not necessarily with perfect strangers. This gap in social ethics indicates a hidden lack of respect and an insincerity in our way of doing things. Furthermore, the politeness we show tends to be on the surface only, while our minds can be internally disrespectful.

We have found at our school that children who are taught to show respect for all others, rather than just superficial politeness, tend to develop true politeness and kindness. Emphasizing that we show respect for others is therefore a way to bring out the true kindness of the human being, and helps to change bad seeds of behavior to good seeds. It works at changing the character of the individual from the root, which is what we ultimately seek. When you respect something then you are being sincere, and when you are simple and sincere you can actually learn something.

If one wants children to perform an activity with care, we have found that this approach of *emphasizing respect* is superior to telling them to "pay attention" or be aware, mindful, careful, or present in the moment. Telling children to concentrate doesn't work as well either, whereas if we say "be respectful," they tend to be careful and focused for the entire length of an activity. We want to train children to be fundamentally diligent and careful in doing things well, and reminding them to be respectful helps in this.

We have tried many approaches and found that emphasizing respect works best in keeping their minds sharp, focused and concentrated on an activity. In emphasizing that the children show respect for everything they do, we have discovered that this teaches self-control, mindfulness and awareness, and it also helps children transform bad tendencies to good tendencies. Therefore we extensively use this approach throughout our school. We train everyone to do everything with a mind of respect, and follow the pattern taught in *The Great Learning* where you must first focus your awareness on some activity, stop your mind from running around, attain non-distraction and mental quiet or calmness in the process of doing, and then you can think and act clearly from within that stillness to achieve the result you want. This entire process of self-cultivation originates from cultivating awareness, and the best way we have found to teach awareness in children is by emphasizing that they *show respect for whatever they are doing*.

As stated, at our school we tried many different ways to get children to pay attention to what they were doing so that they were more careful and focused and thus became better at that activity. We found that if you say, "Pay attention," this doesn't work too well on keeping children focused even though those words would lead you to believe they are having that very effect. If you said, "Be careful," this approach doesn't work too well either. We have tried many other avenues, but so far found that teaching children to have respect works best in teaching focus, awareness, attention and concentration and that this methodology has positive results on countless levels. For some reason it just works best of all the methods we have so far tried although we are always trying something new.

The larger goal is to help children reach a stage where their minds and actions *become unified* in whatever they are doing. Furthermore, it is through concentration that they can perform some task with excellence, which means to the very best of their abilities. Concentration is a skill they will need in life and which we wish them to develop, so you can see that we are once again emphasizing the operating system rather than the software selected to go on the computer. We have found that if we emphasize the angle of having respect for everything, children then pay more attention to all their activities, even simple things such as folding clothes, and tend to perform those tasks better and more carefully because of focus and concentration.

When you do something with respect, you tend to be more alert and your mind and actions tend to both come together in a single point. You tend to bring your mind and body together in that activity, and teaching this mind-body unity is one of our educational goals and objectives. This is a natural result of concentration, and concentration is the sister objective we are after. Even your mind-body coordination skills seem to improve when you are concentrating on something, hence we always tell the children that whatever they do, they should "do it with respect."

We tell the children, "You should do it with your mind there" because we don't want their mind to be lost in wandering thoughts. In this way, children are always taught to pay attention to what they are doing, rather than just mindlessly or mechanically complete certain tasks. In stressing respect, we are basically teaching them concentration and awareness and the responsibility to be careful. You need these skills for life, but these are also the basic skills at the heart of all spiritual training.

Even our teachers need some training to learn to keep this attitude in mind, but the goal is a very noble result that is also referred to in various spiritual traditions as mindfulness, being present, or living in the moment. This type of mindfulness can lead to *samadhi*, which is a mental state of clarity together with inner quiet.

Teaching the children to have respect for what they are doing teaches them how to be conscious human beings in all their activities and aware of all that they are doing. Therefore we tell the children to "eat with respect" or "fold your clothes with respect." We teach them that *their mind must be present and unified with whatever they are doing*, which is cultivating concentration. As stated, if instead we said, "Concentrate!" or "Be careful" or "Pay attention," we have found that this does not achieve the same results at all, so we approach this issue of teaching concentration, or mind-body unification, through the avenue of emphasizing respect. Naturally this methodology is not perfect, but we have found that this approach helps the children to unify their mind-body connection and achieve a higher state of presence during activities than they otherwise would have.

In modern educational terminology, our approach is a secular form of "mindful awareness practices" (MAPs) that support positive developments in children. We want children to learn how to focus and monitor their attention, avoid distraction and control impulses. This requires that they develop connections within the pre-frontal cortex of their brain, which is the area that supports the development of self-reflection and self-regulation. Emphasizing respect helps children calm and unify their bodies and minds and plays a key role in how they learn. Helping children learn how to concentrate, ignore distractions and calm their bodies and minds is something that should play a key role in any educational system.

I have heard that the father of the famous golfer, Tiger Woods, taught him how to ignore external disturbances while he was practicing sinking putts. He wanted his son to learn how to develop total concentration in his golfing and ignore all distractions, so he would make distracting comments while Tiger was about to swing in order to try to break his concentration. Tiger later said this type of concentration practice was one of the reasons he ended up excelling at golf. We don't teach golf at our school, but we do try to teach concentration and try to help the children develop better mind-body coordination in all they do. They have to learn how to develop concentration for ordinary activities as well as for situations that will really need exceptional mental focus in life.

Whether the children at our school are cleaning a table or picking up trash, you will find that we are teaching them to do everything with respect and a delightful heart without complaints or worries or anxieties. We even teach them how to use their chopsticks with respect, and this admonition cuts down on playful chopstick accidents. When children are absent-mindedly following wandering thoughts they are out of a state of presence, and this is when accidents often happen. Accidents usually happen due to poor decision skills or a lack of awareness, but when you emphasize respect, this tends to help the children make better decisions about whatever they are doing and to stay alert with awareness.

If you don't treat objects, people or situations with respect, you can easily cause accidents out of carelessness, so through this mthod we also cut down on accidents that are bound to happen in a school with hundreds of children. Furthermore, if you don't treat things with respect by keeping your mind on what you are doing, you can often create unintended negative consequences through your actions, so thinking things through helps you avoid errors in outcomes too.

We are very keen on having the children learn to think of consequences to their actions, or to appreciate what had to previously happen in order to provide them with their current good fortune, so this method ties right in with this objective. In having respect for all one does, we teach the children to be mindful of the outcomes they achieve and all the good and bad consequences that can arise out of a situation. We also help them link their mind and body (actions) together so they are unified in one whole. That's really what we are striving for.

While how you should hold your chopsticks to eat or how you should place them on the table is a skill, respect is in the mind. Emphasizing respect is focusing on the operating system rather than just emphasizing external skills, which is often a superficial emphasis. Treating things with respect means being mindful of what you are doing. Therefore it actually means mindfulness, focus or concentration, which is a major skill we want the children to develop. It not only means cultivating a state of concern or consideration but cultivating presence and focus.

We are always trying to see if we can upgrade our teaching methods, but this is the best method we have so far found for the idea of helping children to become better at everything, and for transforming bad seeds into better seeds of behavior. In fact, our approach to teaching respect helps them become more appreciative of everything in life, and with appreciation they become more kind, and with kindness they tend to become more respectful. Respect leads to appreciation, appreciation leads to kindness, and kindness leads to respect in a supportive circle of cause and effect.

Once again I wish to stress this finding because I hope it can be used by parents and more schools in our educational system: "Be careful" doesn't seem to produce the same good results as *"Respect what you are doing and put your mind there"* when we have compared the effectiveness of these techniques. We have found that the idea penetrates much deeper and has greater impact than any other method we have tried. You will have to try this for yourself to discover if it is so, and if you ever find a better technique then please tell us so that we can spread it to parents and other educational institutions.

Many other benefits arise from this emphasis on respect. For instance, the principles of respect and kindness are often linked to the idea of *service*, and many people have founded beneficial businesses for society because of the idea of service. Many people have subsequently become rich in life because they held onto an underlying principle of *rendering service to others* as their motivation. Isn't this what we want more of within the world rather than have more people who establish businesses without any higher purpose other than just making money?

As part of teaching children to have respect, we also always ask the children to think deeply about all of the effort that is involved in the fact that they receive or enjoy something. In other words, let's say a student receives a bicycle from their parents. We teach them to think about how their parents had to go to many stores to find just the right bicycle that would match their size and was the color they liked, and how in giving them the bike it meant that their parents had to give up something that they personally wanted to buy for themselves. We try to teach them to think about all the work or sacrifice that goes into getting something they receive, since normally we don't think about these things at all.

In ancient times, people often said you should think about the incredible amount of backbreaking work that goes into the production of a single bowl of rice. Countless people had worked extremely hard for you to be able to eat a bowl of rice, and you were taught to think of all the hard work and toil that went into making that meal possible so that you would thankfully appreciate your food and not waste it. There is a sign posted on our cafeteria wall, which the children look at everyday when they are eating, that reminds them to be appreciative of whatever they have or receive, and in teaching children respect we hope to produce some beneficial results in this way as well:

- It takes the work of ten people to feed one person. Think of all the people that had to plant, grow, harvest, and cook your food – a lot of hard work.
- At home, it takes your whole family to feed you. If you work for the government, the country feeds you. If you eat at school, the entire kitchen staff prepares food for you and teachers serve you. It is not an easy task to feed one person. You must understand this concept.
- In Buddhism, monks use receiving food as an opportunity to reflect on the good things they have done – otherwise they cannot eat. Do they think they deserve the food?
- Emperor Yong Zheng made a law that punished people who wasted food. It didn't matter where you came from – if you wasted food, you would get punished.

Many cultures try to teach people to *be thankful* for what they receive instead of stressing the avenue of respect, but we people often stop being thankful and appreciative after a while and then just start taking things for granted. They don't want to be thankful all the time, and after a while they just ignore those words. It is not that they are ungrateful, but that if you have always had food or clothing or something else then you start taking this abundance for granted, and your expectation is then usually to have more. Rarely do we pause to reflect upon the bounty we now enjoy and perhaps the responsibility to give back and support what made it all possible.

The lack of self-reflection, or introspection, is why people stop taking into consideration the roles others played and efforts they made so that they might be able to enjoy something. People usually just think they personally deserved all the merit that comes to them, but we ask the children to think about whether they actually did enough to merit the things they receive in life. This is good training on a number of levels such as for encouraging conservation, a reduction in desires and appreciation.

If you teach the Confucian habit of *tracing things back to their source* to help grow the attitude of respect, children will tend to become thankful and appreciative of whatever they receive, and will treasure it more and maintain it better. There are many benefits to this, and it also helps us to think of the long-term consequences of whatever we are doing in life through our actions, because those results will be legacies for our children.

A magical thing also starts happening after we teach children to have respect for everything they do. When we teach them to think of everything that goes into their personal merit of having something, after a while their desires for things becomes moderate. They tend to *naturally reduce their desires and be happy with what they have* rather than wallow in dissatisfaction. The pressures of consumerism hammered into us by advertising media, and ideas implanted by TV that you aren't happy unless you have bought the latest gadgets or expensive gifts, therefore don't affect them as much as other children. They can find more peace, happiness and contentment than other individuals without having a lot of material things.

Teaching children to reflect on all the work, care, concern, energy and effort that went into having the things which they now enjoy, actually tends to decrease their desires, because they appreciatively realize all that had to be done for them. They don't become as greedy as other children, but become more appreciative and also more helpful. Our educational method is very different because of this approach in teaching them to always think about what came before and what will come after their behavior.

This type of teaching emphasis goes back to our goal of helping the children train their minds, and is what we call the effort of polishing the mind. We have a saying that "Your mind should be whatever you are doing" which emphasizes the mindfulness and alert awareness aspect of having respect. For instance, one of the famous meditation methods in Buddhism is to just focus on following your breathing. You are supposed to forget about everything else and just focus on watching your breath, which is called "mindfulness of your breathing" practice. When you practice this long enough, you eventually cultivate the ability to be able to concentrate calmly for a long period of time without having scattered thoughts. If wandering thoughts come along, you learn to just ignore them and stay focused in concentration. You become focused, and yet your mind remains clear, calm and peaceful.

With practice you can then bring this skill into regular life so that you can concentrate for a long time on any task and then bring it to completion without much interruption. That ability to concentrate is also a natural result of cultivating a pure or respectful mind that concentrates on the moment, on what you are doing.

In teaching the children to have respect for whatever they are doing, we are teaching them to pay attention to details, be careful, be present in the moment, and produce the results they want. We teach them how to unify their bodies and minds during whatever they are involved with so that all their attention is focused on those activities. There is no cutting of corners to this, so this is connected with teaching them how to do simple tasks correctly, like folding their clothes. This is just one way of polishing the mind and of teaching the mind to be focused on the activity that it is presently engaged in rather than being lost in wandering thoughts.

"Do everything with respect" means giving attention and focus to all your activities. Doing something with respect means that your mind is there on that activity and not wandering about elsewhere. While we call this "respect," it is basically training the mind in mindfulness, awareness, alertness, focus and concentration. It is a life skill that the children should learn that will set them apart from others in a world that has grown crazy with distractions. It is a skill they need to learn not just to preserve their internal peace and sanity, but also so that they can accomplish and achieve things in life. You can only achieve great things if you truly learn to concentrate, and the ability to concentrate taps into an inner place of stillness that is attained when you learn how to ignore distracting thoughts.

Thus we not only teach them to be respectful of what they are doing and thus to focus on what they are doing, but they are trained to think of what it meant that their parents bought them a new pair of shoes. After they learn to think about everything that went into that purchase, such as the sacrifice the parents made, they then tend to be more respectful of their possessions. When they are taught to think of all the energy and effort or sacrifice that went into getting something, this ends up decreasing their desires, and they find themselves thinking more of others and becoming happier with what they have.

When we teach respect along the lines explained, children definitely tend to start appreciating things more. We have found that *from respect comes appreciation*. When the children appreciate things, we can then focus on one of the ultimate goals of education, which is to teach children how to be good people and transform bad habits into better behaviors, such as by transforming evil tendencies to kindness. Let me explain how this works.

Confucius explained that by cultivating yourself you can arrange your family. Families that cultivate themselves can then arrange their state, and states that cultivate themselves can reform the country. Children, for instance, usually mimic their parents' behaviors meaning that if children have bad behavioral traits, sometimes the fault is due to the parents' poor example rather than genes or schooling. The parents' lack of self-cultivation is passed onto the rest of the family by example, and so the family cannot become settled. This is why Confucius said we must inspect ourselves and set good examples for others by first cultivating ourselves. Then others nearby, copying our example, will in turn become more cultivated. We cannot just blame others, such as the school, for the faults of our children because their education starts in the home. As parents, we share in the responsibility for our children's behavior. They are not just influenced by what we teach them, but from observing what we as parents actually say and do. A school cannot work miracles in transforming children's negative behaviors if those behaviors are contradicted in the home environment.

While Confucius said that in cultivating yourself you can end up cultivating your family, state and then changing the world, we have also found a development loop in that teaching respect gives rise to appreciation, appreciation gives rise to kindness, and kindness, in turn, leads to having more respect for others. We thereby set up a **self-reinforcing circle of respect, appreciation and kindness**. We have also found that when the children start changing their behaviors along these lines and go back home, this often influences the entire family to change for the better, so any positive virtues they adopt have the domino effect of transforming the entire family, just as Confucius mentioned.

We really try to focus on respect and kindness at our school. Mencius, who followed in Confucius' footsteps, also said that the path of personal cultivation starts with *goodness and kindness*. We have found that once you teach respect and appreciation then arises, you will tend to become kinder to others and develop a mind of goodness or virtue, so the end result of teaching respect is the kindness we want to see in children rather than the bullying or cruelty we normally hear about in problem children. Our focus on emphasizing kindness and respect is just one of the many ways we try to change bad natures to good ones.

Now in emphasizing respect for whatever they are doing, so that they start to unify their body and mind through concentration, children are also sometimes taught the other side of this, such as what are the direct and indirect *consequences* for when they do things carelessly without respect. This also helps them be more careful when they are doing something. We always try to teach the children to think of the consequences or results of whatever they say or do because this is very good training for the adult world.

As Lieh Tzu (Liezi) taught, men and women in positions of money, power and influence must understand ahead of time what will be the interim and final consequences of whatever they want to try to do in the world, and must understand that they will often face large difficulties, challenges and criticism when they want to accomplish great things. Difficulties and obstructions, including criticism, ridicule and personal attacks, are a natural consequence of trying to do something really great for society and the country. Others may not want to make those same efforts, or will criticize them, but they will certainly arrive later to try and claim any positive fruits as their own.

Lieh Tzu says you must be ready to accept all the criticism you will receive, lies told about you, and troubles you will run into, when you want to do some great deed. This holds even when it comes to performing charity because other people, who are themselves unwilling or incapable of undertaking those same actions, will act as judges quick to criticize your best efforts. It is a characteristic feature of human beings that most people want to criticize other people for efforts while never making an effort themselves. Most people also want to spend your time and money in ways they would not if their own money or efforts were at stake. They want to dictate how you should use *your resources* even though those same people would never sacrifice themselves or their own resources in the same way, or let others have any say over what they personally did. This is a negative aspect of human nature, which Lieh Tzu says you must understand when you want to do great deeds for society.

A personal example comes to mind, from when my family decided to help our grand teacher, Nan Huai-chin, build the Jin-Wen railroad for China.

Even though we believed we would never get our money back for helping China build this railroad, my family decided to undertake this project anyway, even though we only foresaw suffering from our commitment. Everyone said we were crazy for undertaking this project because we had never done anything like this before, and because there were only difficulties to be faced and no personal advantages to be gained other than knowing we had helped. We also knew for certain that despite our desire to serve we would be treated poorly throughout the process, something the press also did to my family after it later discovered we had quietly hosted the first China-Taiwan re-unification talks in Hong Kong. While we were contractually given the rights to buy hundreds of acres of land along the new railway line being built, which everyone openly recognized would be worth hundreds of millions of dollars because of their prime locations, my family flatly refused to cash in on any of these rights because we considered the railroad a social welfare project.

My family has always been committed to supporting Chinese culture and the development of China in various ways, which is why we did not choose to make money from China and take advantage of any of these preferential properties. I don't think many others would have done the same thing. Even though we had this charitable attitude, we were not naive enough to believe that we would not encounter troubles, criticisms, and misrepresentations in helping China to complete this difficult project, which probably would not have been undertaken without our involvement. We were never even thanked by anyone during or upon its completion for making it possible, but we knew it would be this way from the start. Nan Huai-chin had told us that you definitely must quietly suffer all sorts of obstacles, slander, criticism and false rumors if you truly want to help people and society, so we expected this reception, and you will find this teaching in Lieh Tzu where people are criticizing someone's shadow. Lao Tzu teaches all of us to be humble through difficult circumstances, but still committed to any noble purposes in life such as this.

When my family decided to follow the inspiration of our teacher once again and privately build the Taihu Great Learning Center in Miaogang as a place where we could continue to help spread Chinese culture and also put his thoughts into effect, as we had done for over thirty years, we encountered and continue to experience even more difficulties than when helping to finance and build the Jin-Wen railroad. While Lao Tzu teaches that you must be quiet and humble, Lieh Tzu said that when committed to great goals, you must be ready to face obstacles, while remaining true to your own original purposes, despite the difficulties created by others. People reveal themselves by their actions, and you are the only one who can continually guide your own efforts with the same spirit that caused you to undertake those projects in the first place.

A big principle from Lieh Tzu is that you must understand that you will definitely bear sufferings, challenges, criticism and even opposition when you want to accomplish great deeds in life, including attacks by others who lack a giving spirit. While others may be unwilling to undertake those same deeds themselves, they will often be perfectly willing to grab your successes and claim them as their own. You must be realistic about such things in life, and learn how to quietly bear the bad behavior of others while still forging ahead to achieve your objectives. It is a life lesson to recognize that human beings are often greedy for many things such as money, power or influence, and therefore may create troubles for your efforts while using sweet words to hide selfish intentions. Despite what they do, you must stay true to your purposes in life.

This is not just a lesson from Lieh Tzu, but from countless stories of both the Chinese and Western cultures. Therefore, while we don't try to make life at our school difficult for the children at all, from my own personal story we believe that if we never exposed the children to challenging experiences where they might fail or suffer some difficulties and challenges, then we are not properly preparing them for the realities of life and training them how to be able to do great things in the world for their country. Many parents want a school environment without difficulties or the possibility of failure, but this is being unrealistic since the world is not this way. Because obstacles will stand in the way of anyone wishing to accomplish great things in life, you must train children that this is just the way things are, but you must remain optimistic and still undertake the effort.

The normal educational system usually penalizes children for making mistakes, but in the real world you often can only learn by doing, which absolutely involves the necessity of making mistakes. You cannot learn unless you try different things and make mistakes, so you must learn that failure is no big deal. The highest-value jobs, for instance, don't usually come with a lot of instructions but require adaptation and on the job learning. They require "learning agility," which is the ability to pick things up quickly so that you can be thrown into a new situation and thrive. If children grow up afraid to fail at things or make mistakes, they will be at a disadvantage to others who are not afraid to take risks and try many things until they succeed in a big way. Thus, you must teach children how to take intelligent risks and recover quickly when they discover that they have done something wrong.

Another important principle that we try to teach the Taihu School students is how to find the *inherent peace and calmness of their minds*. There is so much pressure in today's fast-paced world that most people tend to develop scattered, wandering minds that are always excessively stimulated and distracted. Just look around you and you will see that this is true, and that few people are finding true internal peace or happiness.

We make it a purpose to try to bring children back to the purity of their minds, the "original you" or true self of the person whose finding brings real peace and contentment. That true self is getting lost underneath all of the stimulation brought on by computers, video games, the internet and the ever increasing pace of life in general. If you think the situation is bad now, just think what it will be in the next few decades, and consider that we must start devising preventive solutions to mental health issues that will surely skyrocket this century. There is a growing health issue from being exposed to the electromagnetic fields (EMF) caused by computers, cell phones and microwave radiation, and definitely a mental health issue from being exposed to too much stimulation.

Chinese culture emphasizes over and over again that the basis of personal cultivation is internal stillness and quiet, so it therefore teaches us how to calm down and adjust ourselves so that we can find that internal bliss. It teaches us how to find the empty purity, calmness or quietness of our minds. Calmness is the root of the human being, which gets clouded by the distractions of wandering thoughts, and since the ultimate root is quietness we try to teach our students how to get back to that inner quietness through various means of self-adjustment. Of all the methods we teach, however, the most powerful method for bringing children back to the purity of their minds is to allow them to have *free time with nature*. This is the big secret we have discovered for helping children touch that internal peace that we are all looking for in life.

Our outside activities allow them free time to just watch the goats or chickens at our school, or look up at the sky, and at those undirected times they can just relax and watch things around them without any mental pressure. They can easily rest or purify their minds in this way. They calm down just from watching everything while being at one with nature. Being with nature gives them a time when they can rest their mind in its natural state without worries or concerns, and thus it is very important to help us achieve our second great goal in education, as grand teacher Nan Huai-chin emphasized.

We don't give the children any special instructions on how to do this. We just let them wander around within the natural settings at our school and they find their own interests without any direction. We have found that they don't need artificial stimulation and excitement all the time, and perhaps many school systems have drifted towards this idea because many children seem bored. I wonder whether they are bored because of how the entire educational system is set up.

For instance, we have had several parents tell us they initially didn't like our rules for keeping children away from television and the internet at the school. However, when they asked their children if they wanted to be transferred to other schools at the end of a semester, prompting them with leading questions such as, "Aren't you bored there?", the children would always respond, "What are you talking about? I'm never bored at the Taihu School. There are always activities going on. It was my other school that I was bored at."

Our children never seem bored at all even when they are just relaxing. We are positive that when they grow up they will never forget this period of calmness and purity which we have tried to give them because many adults tell us their own experiences of what they remember in childhood and talk of instances like this. In short, we try to create a safe space, a sanctuary removed from all the hustle and bustle of the world where children are free of artificial, polluting influences and can find this internal peace so that they can always know it. People may argue that this is not realistic, but it certainly has value and our parents say it is indeed transformative.

Once again, our method is that we try to show the children a way home to the inherent purity of their minds *through nature*. This is how we try to help them experience the purity and calmness of their minds. It is not an exciting happiness or joy we are talking about, but something very clear, calm and comfortable from being at peace with oneself and in touch with nature. We strive to give children this experience so that they will always remember it and, knowing that it is available, will learn how to retrieve it when they need it.

People may think that constant stimulation and excitement is important for learning, but we believe this is not correct. Real learning takes place when the mind is calm and quiet, and that state of concentration is when one's real wisdom can come out. This is a bedrock principle of Chinese culture, but in copying Western intellectual trends over the last few centuries we have tended to drift away from this emphasis. Teaching the inherent purity of the mind is actually *one of the main purposes of education* rather than the constant stimulation espoused by modern educational theorists. The academics on this matter definitely have it backwards.

Our grand teacher, Nan Huai-chin, emphasized to us time and time again that this goal of *leading people to the purity of their minds* should be one of the two major goals in education, and you can see it in the world (or hear it in our parents' stories) that everyone is seeking some sort of internal peace and contentment today but just cannot find it. You can only find it within your mind, so we do our best to make sure children can taste that experience so they can always retrieve it later in life and we try to teach the children how they can adjust their minds and bodies to achieve it whenever they feel out of balance. Our big secret, however, is that we have found that experiencing nature is the best way to help them touch this internal peace, stillness, calmness and contentment. This is another of the many reasons why we emphasize so many outdoor activities on our campus.

SAMI KUO & BILL BODRI

4

EDUCATIONAL GUIDANCE FROM
THE GREAT LEARNING

Much of what guides us at our school are the ideas espoused by Confucius in *The Great Learning*. Within *The Great Learning*, Confucius said that the primary goal in life is to learn how to find oneself so as to become a true human being, and teaching the children how to do this, or laying the foundations so that they can do this later in life, is the underlying purpose of our school. As educators we want to prepare the children so that they have the teachings, skills and mindset by which they can find themselves in life and thus carve out a self-reliant career that lets them be themselves and contribute to society.

To find your true self and become a true human being, Confucius said you must accomplish three goals. This entails a lifelong pursuit that is called the "great learning," and so we aim to help our students lay the foundations for this great task in what and how we teach at our school. As stated, we are not just interested in teaching skills and knowledge as all schools do, but also in preparing individuals to be able to achieve the three goals of *The Great Learning*, which Confucius taught should be lifelong goals for all human beings.

In other words, at our school we help children to lay the foundations for a lifetime of self-cultivation if they so choose to take on that task. We prepare

68

them by giving them familiarity with the proper skills and teachings so that they can later succeed in the task of self-cultivation and accomplish the three humanistic goals of Confucianism that are also found within Buddhism and Taoism and other spiritual paths.

We can speak about two different levels of meaning for goals espoused within *The Great Learning*. At one level it is talking about the great task for all human beings to find their original nature, or true self, and to understand that this true nature is their "beingness" of existence. This search for your true self is the "great learning" that we all must strive for within this lifetime, and that search is called the "process of self-cultivation."

The Chinese say that whether you are an emperor or a common person, self-cultivation is the one fundamental thing you must do in this life, which is to work at the task of searching for your "true self" or self-nature. This is the lifelong process that Confucius called the "great learning." If you find your true self, which is the "bright virtue" of Confucianism, you have then succeeded in attaining the enlightenment of Buddhism and have also become the "cultivated person" or "true man" of Taoism. If you accomplish this great undertaking, Jewish culture says you become a "righteous man," Islam says you become "perfect," and Chinese culture says that you become a "sage."

To accomplish this feat, the first step is we must cultivate ourselves to find the inner peace of our mind. We must learn to know inner calmness, stillness or silence. This is a foundational step to being able to find our inherently pure "bright virtue," which means our true self or fundamental nature. "Bright virtue" refers to our original nature that is the purity of our mind before anything is added to it and before it is stirred by any outside influences.

The task of searching for this "bright virtue" of our mind is also called "cultivating virtue," so you can see how teaching children to find the inner quiet and calm center of the mind, which is a cardinal principle of Chinese culture, and how teaching them to be virtuous human beings are both tied up with the concepts within *The Great Learning*.

The second principle of *The Great Learning* is that once you understand what is your true mind, then you have to learn how to use it to function in the world in all situations, and most of all in beneficial interactions with other people. You must become devoted to helping other people, which often means teaching them. Once you find your true nature, you have to make that realization work in regular life by integrating it with compassionate, helpful activities for others. This means spreading what you understand to other people such as by teaching them and guiding them in other ways. Once you have found your bright virtue, you must use what you understand by spreading its positive influences throughout human culture.

In Chinese culture, many people leave home to cultivate the Tao (attain enlightenment). After they attain the Tao, usually they then go out into the world to help society, but this part of their story is not written down because people take this result as natural in Chinese culture. What you do for society is actually the *Tao part* of "attaining the Tao" (attaining enlightenment), whereas people who focus on just the cultivation aspect of experiencing wondrous *gong-fu* results demonstrate selfishness and greediness because they never engage in any great contributive deeds for others.

If you work hard, then whether you take heaven's road or the devil's road of cultivation, you will still attain self-cultivation *gong-fu*, or inner results, so this aspect of personal cultivation is not the Tao. The "Tao part" of self-cultivation is working on cultivating virtue and benefitting society, which is what Confucius emphasized. When Tzu Kung asked Confucius, "What would you think of an individual who gave extensively to the common people and brought help to everyone?", Confucius replied, "If you wanted to describe such an individual, 'sage' would probably be the right word to use."

When we compare Confucius' example and his teachings on doing many things to help society, this is very close to the Mahayana Buddhist idea of compassionately working to help others, and the result is huge merit because of helping so many people. Naturally we want our children to grow up to be contributive to society rather than just people who just selfishly consume whatever is available, or whose actions leave misfortune in their wake.

The final principle is that once you have attained enlightenment and start working to help others, you should never stop until you reach a state of ultimate goodness in any situation. For instance, you should always try to be as good as you can be and try to make any situation as good as it can be, too. You should do your best without regard for success or failure. Confucius' words also encapsulate the principle of *vigor* and commitment in continuing to work until you accomplish some goal. In your engagement with the world along these lines, you must also not go too far in your actions but should stop at the optimal point for any situation. You keep working until you achieve the highest possible good, and then you can stop. All your actions in life should embody wisdom, and so you should always keep working until you achieve your desired objectives.

Just as the Greeks advised that you should cultivate a "golden mean" in everything you do, and just as a mind emptying of thoughts reaches a point of cessation or inner quiet called "stopping," every situation has a perfect stopping point and you should not exceed it by going too far. However, you should certainly work to make every situation as good as possible, which is the third Confucian goal of never stopping until you reach the highest good. With every action you do, you should stop at just the right effect without going overboard, which is what Buddhism calls applying wisdom to your actions. For instance, ordering people about *only at the proper time* is an example of this particular virtue.

A second level of meaning to *The Great Learning* is that we can view it solely according to human virtues rather than according to the great calling of finding your true self or original nature, such as you also find emphasized in Chinese Buddhism or Taoism. There is a metaphysical aspect to the text, and more mundane aspects, too. At this level of meaning, the first emphasis in *The Great Learning* is still that you should strive to understand what bright virtue is, only now we are talking about the virtue or correctness of human actions in any situation rather than the root source of the mind. You should understand what goodness and virtue mean for all the common situations in the everyday world, and try to achieve that.

We definitely want our children to grow up being good human beings rather than rascals and criminals who don't know right from wrong and who lack any conscience. We definitely want our children to exhibit all the good virtues there are, so at the Taihu School we try to teach them what it means to cultivate virtuous behavior and how to be good human beings.

Cultivating proper, kind, and considerate behavior is one of the everyday goals for human beings. Even manners, such as polite eating or not talking during movies or standing in front of a moving line, are matters of propriety we should be teaching children. *The Essential 55*, by Ron Clark who won a Disney Teacher of the Year award for his educational efforts, offers some interesting classroom ideas for teaching proper behavior.

Another point is that after you understand what virtue, goodness and propriety are, you should cultivate this in yourself and in your relationships with others. You must even treat objects virtuously, which is why we teach children to "show respect" for all their activities. More importantly, they are taught that they should interact with other people according to the proper standards of virtue and good conduct such as being responsible, reliable, honest and trustworthy. Confucius said that virtue should guide the nature of your relationships with other people, and so we try to teach this at our school so that children don't grow up and think it's okay to do bad or evil things in the world. You must interact with others along the ethical lines of propriety, and what you should hope to accomplish together should represent virtuous objectives as well.

In the West people often say they want their children to be "spiritual," but in Chinese culture we more properly say we want our children to "be virtuous" because practicing virtue and being a good person is the *basic foundation* of being spiritual. For instance, having respect for your parents and elders means taking care of them, and this is included within the ideal of proper behavior and cultivating virtue. While this is not normally considered as "being spiritual," in practicing this type of virtuous concern you are indeed cultivating a spiritual life.

Cultivating virtue is not being religious but humanistic, and yet it produces a spiritual result. The natural result of cultivating virtue and goodness is therefore called "spiritual cultivation," so once again we all need to be cultivating our "bright virtue" in this life, which is the task of self-cultivation. Whether we talk of the Chinese cultural treasures of Buddhism, Taoism, Confucianism or its other philosophical schools, *they all emphasize the importance of cultivating virtue and correct behavior.* Even Chinese Taoism, when its name is properly translated into English, means "the Way of Virtue." This idea of cultivating virtue as the foundation of the spiritual life is found in Western religions, too, including Christianity, Judaism and Islam. It is the core essence of the primary educational objective of teaching people how to be good human beings, so we emphasize this at our school.

Lastly, even when we are being virtuous, Confucius warned that we should never go too far with our actions and behaviors. With everything we do, we must find a harmonious stopping point and avoid extremes. For every activity we should know when to stop, for there is a point beyond which we have gone too far. While we should act with vigor to achieve our goals, all our actions and behaviors should not overreach. We should not extend beyond a proper stopping point that tries to achieve the highest good for any situation. We should not stop until we achieve a virtuous objective, and when we achieve it we can then halt our efforts and rest.

There is even an optimum stopping point when it comes to being virtuous. For instance, if parents show too much love for a child and therefore never scold them or punish them for their mistakes, those children can easily grow up to be criminals because they were never corrected. Chinese culture has many admonishing tales on this principle of how virtues taken to extremes become vices, and how uncorrected vices can become malignancies on society. Of course there are also stories of how negative behaviors in certain circumstances can represent virtues, such as getting angry at people in order to prevent them from great wrongdoing. The main principle, however, is that there is always a point past which something becomes an extreme, and then it becomes its opposite just as Taoism always warns. Confucius taught that we must learn to reach an optimum balance point that satisfies needs, and which represents the right solution in solving our call for action in the first place. By going just far enough without going overboard, we eliminate mistakes.

In the West this is similar to the idea of avoiding hubris (the arrogance of going too far) that the Greeks adopted for their culture. This idea of avoiding hubris can readily be seen in Greek tragedies and its histories such as Thucydides' *The History of the Peloponnesian War*. Similar ideas can be found in Plutarch's *Lives of the Noble Greeks and Romans*, which even today still serves as a valuable lesson on moral virtues and vices. It teaches about the influence of character on the lives and destinies of men.

The Greeks also promoted the idea of achieving a "golden mean" for all situations. Just as Confucius taught that you should not be deficient or excessive in your actions, the Greeks felt that you should practice proportionate balance in all your activities, too, for as Daedalus warned his son Icarus, you must "fly the middle course." Even at the Temple of Delphi there was a carving that said, "Do nothing in excess." The Confucian ideal of stopping at the ultimate "virtue point" of a situation has similarities to ideas within Greek philosophy, Christianity, Taoism, Buddhism, and many other spiritual traditions.

This general idea of optimal balance, harmony or moderation is therefore something that both Eastern and Western cultures agree upon although there are indeed differences between their concepts and their execution. There are many overlaps between the ideals of proper behavior, but few people bother to study such things. For instance, the idea of "righteousness" in Chinese culture also means appropriateness, which also carries the Confucian meaning of not going too far. Confucius had a saying that "trustworthiness is close to righteousness," so there are linkages to this idea as well.

There is an optimum stopping point to every action that addresses a condition where the action doesn't extend itself into becoming excessive or extreme. Courage, for instance, can either turn into recklessness or cowardice when it goes too far in either direction. When you harbor too many desires or your mind becomes too distracted, these mental excesses represent harmful imbalances too. Consuming too much due to the cultural influences of consumerism is also an unhealthy extreme as is the idea of trying to make money while destroying the environment. This is just making the world worse off and the opposite of the Chinese ideal of harmony. Confucius said that the ultimate or perfect point of stopping produces stability and calmness, and that is what we must strive to cultivate. He also said that we must learn how to draw this principle into our worldly actions. That calmness is like reaching a peak on a mountain where your mind becomes unfettered, open, empty and free.

Even Buddhism, using the simile of tuning the strings on a musical instrument, discusses the idea that you shouldn't go too far in any direction. If those strings are too taut or too loose then they won't produce the right sound, meaning that your actions should always be balanced and proper.

You have to tune the strings of a musical instrument to a point that is just right—not too taut or loose—and then stop there without going to an extreme in either direction. This idea, along with the idea of thinking about consequences, even lies at the foundation of how to develop government and social policy for a country's benefit.

Confucius also explained that if you can cultivate awareness then you can achieve stillness in your mind, and then calmness. He said that when you stop following wandering thoughts by knowing your mind and watching it with mindfulness, you can stabilize your mind and then reach a state of inner calm. Mental calmness leads to internal peace, and because of that peaceful state of mind you can finally be able to really think clearly. Everything we can know is because of our thinking, and when your mind is clear, calm and undistracted then your thinking and decision-making can be at their absolute best.

This Confucian sequence of cultivating awareness, stopping or stillness, calmness and then clarity ties everything together. It is the foundational basis for being able to cultivate correct thinking and achieving any result you want in life. If you practice learning mental calmness through introspection, you can eventually cultivate a clear mind and attain internal peace. When your mind becomes quiet, you can then think clearly and correctly. Through proper thinking you can come to correct conclusions about how to achieve some particular result you want, and all these factors, and more, are embodied in our special educational method.

This is why we try to create a special learning environment at our school free of distractions so that the children can learn how to delve deeply into topics without being rushed. Even the length of our classroom sessions is designed as a method of helping children be able to achieve states of concentration. Through concentration they can have clear minds and learn how to focus on the tasks at hand, and in quiet stability they also learn how to think better because they are not distracted. Basically, when children learn how to be calm, mindful, and respectful when doing something, they develop a little bit more towards achieving a clear mind of concentration that can think and focus clearly.

Previously we discussed that the idea of *cultivating respect* contains the principles of awareness, mindfulness, carefulness, quiet, focus, consideration, appreciation, kindness, concentration and presence all bundled up together. When you cultivate the mindset of respect, it is easier to fathom the result of any actions you might take, and you will thereby produce better results and outcomes in life. It sounds so easy to say "Be respectful," but you have to continually train children to cultivate this type of awareness, quiet, focus and concentration until it becomes a habitual way of using their mind, and then their inherent wisdom for how to do things properly will start coming out.

Even for adults this is hard, which is why we see so many crazy things being developed in the world today. People create all sorts of destructive influences, especially television programs, without thinking about the effects they are producing on society. This tendency is because people are for the most part no longer respectful of the consequences of their actions. If you want to lead people to happiness or prepare them for handling great responsibilities in the world, such as training them to be leaders who can ask the right questions and make good decisions, you need to teach them how to respect things and people starting from when they are children.

We all want our children to be able to make better choices and decisions in life. The world ahead of them is literally filled with choices and decisions. Life is entirely dependent on our choices and decisions in the end. How do you prepare children for the fact that they will have to make countless decisions in life that will affect their future? Is it by giving them more knowledge and skills or is it by first training the mind itself—the organ of thinking—in how it should properly function, such as by emphasizing the wisdom of the Chinese and Western cultures? We definitely feel that the time-tested wisdom of Chinese culture, whose humanistic principles are recognized in other spiritual traditions as well, should serve as the underlying processing system and guidance mechanism for our decisions and actions.

We believe we should help children train their minds to have good habits, so we focus on this task of teaching them how to polish their minds at our school. We try to teach them how to correct their own mental conduct because thinking is behavior that has not yet become manifest. In terms of the spiritual field, it is said that you cannot attain high spiritual states if your mental activity has not yet been transformed, so we teach our children the basics of how they can adjust themselves in many different ways to accomplish this. We also believe that we should help enable their inherent wisdom to come out, and are devoted to transmitting to them the several thousand-year-old wisdom of Chinese culture that has been developed by our sages and tested by history.

Confucius also commented, "I broaden myself with culture and restrain myself with proper standards of behavior," and felt that character and being a good example were far more effective in helping individuals be good people than using laws and punishments to deter bad actions. This is also a good summary of some of the functions of our school. We certainly teach children many skills and knowledge, but we place a particular emphasis on teaching them how to use their mind and how to adopt the best of Chinese culture into their lives. We try to help them establish mind habits that will serve them their entire lives for whatever they decide to do, but also wish to give them the rich cultural content, whether from the East or West, that will help them find a higher life purpose and live a happy life of meaning, impact and consequence.

5
TRANSMITTING CHINESE CULTURE
THROUGH THE CLASSICS

You have heard us consistently emphasize that the special focus at our school is on teaching Chinese culture. Some people ask us, "What is culture, and why are you focusing on Chinese culture rather than Western ideals at your school? As an international school, shouldn't you focus more on Western culture, especially as it is so predominant nowadays?"

To us, culture is a particular living style or way of living. It is not just a body of knowledge that you study as a topic, but a way of life. Culture is a way of living life and doing things in a certain way with a certain mindset, philosophy or perspective. Chinese culture, for instance, has developed over thousands of years and has the particular characteristic of incorporating a special wisdom for life that involves cultivating internal and external harmony, kindness, benevolence, and concern for bringing about auspicious outcomes in the world. It has many wonderful characteristics that are too numerous to mention.

Western cultural values also stress many wonderful things, but do not necessarily emphasize the same principles as in Chinese culture. In the world's various spiritual traditions you will find a consistent emphasis on wisdom and calmness and we feel that Chinese culture, of all the world cultures, embodies these two principles best in regular life.

Chinese feel that living a life of inner peace and contentment while still striving to make things better, and performing activities according to wisdom rather than mere intelligence, will bring out the best results of peace, harmony and happiness for all participants. It will produce the best result of the real happiness in life that Chinese call "pure clear fortune."

When you look at the Chinese classics deeply you will discover that they, too, are focused on trying to lead people to the best in life and the inherent goodness or kindness of the human being. This is the basis of Chinese culture in that it truly focuses on having us develop the virtuous aspects of our character and build positive, balanced relationships with other people and the world. Chinese culture focuses on how you should be a good/virtuous person in the world in terms of your mind and behavior, and emphasizes acts of merit you should perform for your family, society and country.

To transmit Chinese culture, which has maintained what has worked over thousands of years while getting rid of what hasn't, we therefore particularly emphasize the Chinese classics since they embody the best of what Chinese culture has to offer. When we were first developing our school, we formulated a curriculum based on the guidance of our grand teacher, Nan Huai-chin, who would often point out the best aspects of Chinese culture that we should emphasize for young children, and this is how we started to develop our progression of materials that children should sequentially study.

We teach all the standard Chinese classics, and each of the Classics has a different type of emphasis. We teach the **"nine classics"** at our school because they represent the core of Chinese cultural values. Within these classics you can learn how to write a poem, how to deal with people issues, what strategies to use in various situations, and historical lessons too.

The Chinese classics all have unique purposes, but a common bond is that they were written to help lead people to the best there is in life, and also encourage us to do things for good purposes. In the West you might say that they help lead people to a golden mean in outcomes where everything is in balanced harmony, and Chinese take this as "best" rather than the Western idea of just maximizing everything to reach short-sighted "optimum" states that are unsustainable. For instance, the Chinese appreciate humility and moderation because these ideals enable one to preserve a state of goodness for a long period of time without it degrading, whereas the Western idea of maximization does not necessarily lead to either balance or long-term prosperity. The problem with maximization principles is that they often lead to eventual extremes that cannot be maintained over the long run.

Now no matter what the ultimate level of wealth, power and position in society, everyone must strive to cultivate the same objectives of being a good person and doing things in a wise way for auspicious results and good purposes. This is the viewpoint that is transmitted throughout the Chinese classics. This ideal is different from the legalistic or efficiency ideas in the West where a company might rape the earth, and pollute all the land and residents in an area, in order to simply make some quick profits, and then walk away without feeling any responsibilities to society or the environment if their actions are perfectly legal. Western development has led to companies being run by leaders without any moral conscience or public values. As long as something is profitable and permitted, it is pursued.

The Western idea is best expressed as, "What's in it for me, right now, and how can I get the most out of it as quickly as possible?" For instance, certain companies want to patent human genes, or patent nature, simply because they can make money from doing this. They don't ask if this is right in principle, but just focus on the economic aspect of this desire. They want to ignore the fact that the *eventual consequences* from this course of action will be destructive to humanity as a whole, but they don't want to even think about this because there is money to be made. If it is legal they will just do it, and cite the profit motive that entices more research and development as the reason we should allow this.

This is not just unwise but will be extremely harmful in terms of all the eventual consequences, so Chinese culture cannot agree with this type of nonsense. Because of capitalism unchecked by wisdom and the principles of virtue, righteousness and benevolence, a destructive pattern of measuring humanity or actions solely in terms of money and material outcomes has slowly developed in the West. We have all drifted away from the humanistic values that are the stuff of life because societies now rate the desire for profits over the importance of kindness and wisdom.

While we try to teach Chinese cultural principles through all our activities at the school, the most concentrated form of instruction is transmitted through the literature of the Chinese classics. There are three primary avenues by which we teach this material.

The first teaching method we use is **recitation**. Every student needs to recite thirty-six specially selected books that have important content from Chinese culture. My family developed these books nearly a decade ago after carefully considering all sorts of source materials, and now due to our earlier charitable efforts they are used by over eight million children throughout China. Along the way we have received many wonderful stories from parents about the results that recitation has produced in helping children transform their behaviors from bad to good, but we cannot go into this here. We have, in the past, run entire conferences on many aspects of this method, and still offer them from time to time.

In our recitation classes, the children don't need to understand what they are reciting, but must simply recite these thirty-six classics. At our school they recite 40 minutes in the morning, 20 minutes after lunch, and sometimes 30 minutes after dinner. I cannot go into all the details, which we sometimes discuss at seminars, but only wish to say that we have found tremendous results from having children recite these books.

We also teach all the **government requirements** for literature classes at our school, which is our second method of instruction. The government has standards for what it also wants children to learn about the classics and about Chinese literature and history, and so of course we always make sure the children learn all this as well.

Third, we teach the **explanations of the classics**, which is separate from just having children recite them. This is where we once again differ from the curriculum in most Chinese schools. We believe in teaching children how to interpret the classics on their own so that they can always do this for any ancient book, rather than just provide them with the meaning of the classics that they should memorize. We are not trying to overwhelm them with knowledge but give them an operating system that enables them to unravel the meaning of the classics on their own. Hence, while we explain the classics to them, we also progressively teach them how to interpret the classics on their own, because this is a skill we want them to develop and be able to use throughout their lives.

In terms of "explaining the classics," we also try to provide the students with a perspective that enables them to see how to match this wisdom with their regular life, and this is what we focus on explaining. In particular, we want the children to be able to develop their own ideas on the deeper meaning of Chinese culture and start to use them. We want to wean them away from depending on other people's interpretations of the classics and want them to think about how to incorporate these lessons into their own lives. To do this we train them using a special sequential process we developed that slowly enables them to be able to interpret the meaning of any Chinese classical text they may come upon.

For instance, based on Nan Huai-chin's suggestions, our 1st and 2nd graders are taught the *Chian Tzu Wen* (Thousand Character Classic). The 3rd and 4th graders are taught the *You Xue Cong Ling* (Encyclopedia of Chinese Classics), which is like an encyclopedia of Chinese culture. The 5th and 6th graders are taught the *Gu Wen Guan Zhi* (Collection of Classical Essays), which contain history and stories.

Through this progression of books and our other materials, the children slowly develop the skill of being able to interpret ancient classical texts on their own. Of course we also explain the meaning of the classics to the children, but we want the children to develop their own opinions. If the students do not learn how to read and interpret classics on their own, then our nation will slowly lose the ability to retrieve Chinese culture. Furthermore, we place a special emphasis on teaching the children how to match the topics within the classics with their way of doing things. We want to teach them how to apply the means of personal thinking and cultivation revealed within the classics to their regular life, otherwise all the study and familiarization merely amounts to useless bookwork. This pragmatic emphasis on "living the classics" is another way in which we differ from the way the classics are typically taught in most Chinese schools.

If you want to understand the classics you can simply use a dictionary to look up all the words and then you will know the meaning of the text. However, because we feel that Chinese culture is a way of life, we emphasize how the life-wisdom of our ancestors has been codified in this literature and the fact that it is our task in life to retrieve that wisdom through understanding and make it part of the way we actually *do things*. We try to bring the meanings of any text into the real world by explaining how its message should affect our behavior.

This is how we try to transmit Chinese culture to the new generation, fulfilling our grand teacher's hope that the greatness of Chinese culture is not lost over time, and thus give children a foundation not ordinarily established by the present Chinese school system. We hope that one day, in turn, they will be able to pass this sort of knowledge onto their own children, strengthening the culture through the process over time. We firmly believe that this foundation will help them to live better lives and to make better decisions in the world regardless of their ultimate positions in society. Furthermore, we are absolutely convinced that this route will help produce an even greater China because many countries have been destroyed when they lost sight of their original cultural values and history.

A story comes to mind that illustrates the difference of our approach to teaching the Chinese classics. One day, one of our new teachers from the public school system started explaining the meaning of a classical passage to his class. A student in class then raised her hand and said, "Teacher, I am very sorry to stop you. Can you tell me something that is not in the book because I already read the stories by myself."

It's funny to hear this coming from a child, but our children are already trained to be able to read and understand the meaning of the texts on their own because of the particular books we have them study. We train them to develop their own understanding of the meaning rather than have to depend on someone else's interpretations, and do so by teaching them how to seek information on their own and independently think for themselves. If you are in business you will certainly have to read many reports and need to learn how to interpret these materials for yourself or seek new information. As they get older, the children exposed to our method will have no problem unraveling the meanings of other classical works because of how we have trained them, and they won't have to wait until they are adults before they start understanding these other cultural treasures. We teach them to first recite the classics in order to lay a foundation so that they are later able to critically think about them.

Of course, understanding is just a portion of what we want them to master. We particularly want the children to be able to *bring the meaning of the stories into their regular life* because once again, knowledge to us is only a kind of special software, and you cannot use it as a computer's operating system. It is the basic operating system (way of thinking) that is important for their lives, and we hope to give the children one of the best processing models possible by teaching them the best of Chinese culture. We feel that Chinese culture itself should be the operating system for the children *because it actually represents a way of life* rather than just a topic to be studied. Therefore we try to bring out this way of life and its principles in our classes so that the children can integrate the lessons into their own lives.

Naturally we also teach them the best from Western culture and civilization because this is one of our fundamental principles as an international school, and it is just good common sense. As Nan Huai-chin instructed, we are always trying to integrate the best of the East with the best from the West, and the entire Taihu Great Learning Center is based on this principle of forging a new type of unified cultural thought. This doesn't mean that we should just blindly copy all that comes from the West without looking at the results its philosophies have produced. This was a mistake China made when it first started opening up in the 1980s, but now most people know better and are in many fields looking for better solutions than what the West is currently using.

It would be beneficial for the Chinese to copy the Western habit of careful research, analysis and deep study before instituting policy changes in various fields, such as in business or government. Far too many leaders within Chinese organizations simply want all their random opinions to become policy after they gain power, and rarely try to scientifically study issues to determine what is the best course of action. Drunk with power but lacking common sense and concern, bosses too often order their staff to try to complete tasks in ways that go against the laws of physics. While we laugh at these stories, we should understand that this demonstrates a great weakness of the psyche that we need to correct through our educational system. Our future leaders need an educational system that will not only teach them how to confront difficult problems and make much better decisions, but that instills within them a sense of responsibility that is greater than a sense of entitlement.

When a new leader institutes an errant policy that doesn't work out, people mistakenly refuse to correct the error because they take the original errant decision, having come from "the boss," as being something sacred even though wrong. These tendencies, together with the Chinese leanings that most people want to act like the boss, are a stumbling block for developing large organizations that can avoid great errors, continue to incorporate an ideal of benevolence, and last for several generations.

As Nan Huai-chin indicated, we definitely need to study the Western ideals on professional *management* to help uplift the Chinese culture in this area. We should not produce adults who will not question authority or the status quo, or who unthinkingly assimilate what they are told and act accordingly, because this is an approach of stupidity that is fraught with countless errors. Furthermore, we cannot always put the materialistic pursuit of profits and the good life above everything else. China's Grand Historian, Sima Qian, was once reading about a famous conversation on enriching a country that Mencius had with the King of Liang, and aptly commented "the pursuit of profit is truly the beginning of disorder. This is why Confucius seldom spoke of profit, always strengthening the source."

In any case, in the choice between Western and Eastern values, we feel that the foundational value system for a Chinese educational system should be primarily based on deep Chinese cultural principles that are reiterated over and over again by our sages, rather than Western ideals. However, we are committed to incorporating both of these ideals into a new Chinese educational model that is stronger than either separately.

If you go to a typical international school for children, it might say that the goal of the school is to raise children to be able to accept different cultural values and ideas, as well as the normal expectation that the children should be able to develop great interpersonal skills and think independently. Our standpoint is that we must help to set up a foundational system of *values first* before we expose the children to all sorts of other competing cultural values, otherwise this might possibly confuse them. Traditional Chinese wisdom and values are a wonderful operating system, and should not in any way be viewed as second place to those of the Western world.

You have to think about the root and result of what you want to achieve when you found a school, and after deep consideration our focus is set on having Chinese cultural values as our foundation. Once that foundation is communicated to the children and becomes established, then it becomes easier for the children to accept values from many other cultural systems that we also introduce to them, such as teachings from Indian, American or European culture. For instance, we celebrate holidays from many different cultures at our school, but the Chinese culture always remains at the core.

In short, we feel that the great wisdom of the Chinese culture has been embodied in the Chinese classics, and those books have lasted throughout countless centuries precisely because everyone recognizes that they contain great wisdom. We want to transmit that wisdom to our children so that they can do great things for the world and live richer, fuller, happier lives. However, if you just teach the meaning of these works without teaching how to link that wisdom with your own actions and life in general, it becomes just another bit of stale knowledge that will get thrown away in life. It will just remain knowledge that is never used that won't improve your life at all. The cultural information and perspective we provide to children has to be relevant and useful, and should become integrated with their lives, and so we strive to transmit the best of Chinese cultural thinking to the children and teach them *how to use it*. Once we have established the Chinese cultural perspective on a firm basis, we then add on the best we find from anywhere else to the curriculum so that there is a merging of Eastern and Western philosophies.

Our primary goal is to give children a strong Chinese foundation *first* that will enrich and improve their life all through their adulthood, so we especially strive to bring out the meaning and flavor of our classical treasures so that they can benefit from them. We try to teach them how to match that information with their daily living, such as how to live in harmony with nature according to the Chinese system of the twenty-four seasons of the year, so they can make use of all these treasures into their adulthood. We hope that our method can strength people's innate sense of virtue, and imprint an appreciation of cultural thought that is deep enough that they will later pass their understanding onto their own children, thus slowly improving the nation at large and helping it progressively grow stronger as the generations go by. This is how our way of teaching the classics differs from what is found in most schools, and it gives you some idea of the results we hope to help accomplish by this new method.

6
TEACHING RESPONSIBILITY
AND SELF-RELIANCE

To accomplish our larger mission of helping children learn courage, independence, self-responsibility and self-reliance, our school teaches them how to perform various life skills such as how to clean their clothes, clean their rooms, how to walk, stand, or even dress themselves properly for the weather and seasons, how to greet guests, eat politely, grow a garden and so on. Some of what we do along these lines comes from Western science, from our familiarity with teaching methods that we admire from other countries, from other boarding school methods, and once again from Chinese culture too.

In general, Chinese children today tend to be given too much freedom or are overly spoiled. While many in the older generation have grown up experiencing deep suffering, out of love for their children and grandchildren they wish to remove all forms of deprivation from their lives and make their lives very easy. The one child policy complicates matters further, and thus single sons or daughters are rarely taught to take responsibility for doing simple household chores now, but they really should because they will end up doing them later in life. Parents are unfortunately becoming slaves to the wishes of their children, absolving them of such responsibilities, and think this is showing parental love. Everything is done for the children so they don't have to think for themselves or even learn simple life skills.

Since the parents and grandparents on both the father's and mother's side are all spoiling this present generation of children, what will the future of the nation be if this continues? The truth is that the rise and fall of nations rests in the hands of its citizens, and if we train our children incorrectly, we jeopardize the nation's future. We don't want our children to feel incapable and lack confidence because they have never been trained how to do simple things to take care of themselves. Therefore we put special emphasis on correcting this at our school by teaching basic life skills.

We can contrast our present day situation in China with early American and European traditions where children were given great responsibilities even when they were young. They were even involved in important professional activities at a young age because of the American apprenticeship craft system or the European Renaissance studio system where work and learning were integrated. This type of project learning was put at the heart of the educational system rather than put at the edges, which is why we have a lot of hands-on activities at our school. We certainly want to teach our children how to become more independent, more responsible, and how to survive through self-reliance without being a burden on others, but how can we do this in a manner appropriate for today?

Teaching self-responsibility has been done for countless generations in China, and it is only recently that we have abandoned this pattern. The one child policy has caused parents to now start doing everything for their children so that the concept of teaching self-reliance has been thrown out of the window. Doing everything for your children is not the proper way to teach them how to grow up to be independent. Therefore we have devised a system of personal responsibility training, in conjunction with our martial arts, life skills and outdoor activities, which actually prepares them early in life to be able to manage things on their own and to live in the world without becoming a burden on others.

The children at our school not only learn how to clean their clothes, tidy their rooms, greet guests, serve tea or food to others and so on but learn how to do everything well and without complaint. Chinese children have been doing these simple tasks for generations to help the family, and one day these habits they learn will certainly in turn be passed onto their own children. Thus we try to help transmit the good habits of living to the next generation.

A unique aspect to our school is not just the strong teacher-student bond that comes from living together, but the fact that the children are even paired off and assigned to **"shr-tu" ("sifi-tudi" older-younger) senior-junior student-student relationship** where they learn to take care of one another with older children taking care of and teaching the younger children. It is just like having older brothers and sisters taking care of the younger ones in the same family, but it is much more formalized so that this actually happens rather than just wishing it would happen! The older student is always helping the younger in a fraternal teacher-pupil type relationship, and the system teaches compassionate concern and regard for others.

Many one-child problems that plague China disappear because of this influence, and many children tell us they cannot wait until the following school year when they will be old enough to become an older brother ("ge-ge") or older sister ("mei-mei") themselves. Our system emphasizes always taking care of one another like this and it helps the children learn kindness, compassion and concern for other people.

You must also consider that if children learn to take care of others, they are not growing up in a totally self-centered fashion but are also learning the basics of *filial piety*. If they learn how to take care of others now, they will also recognize their responsibility to properly take care of their parents later in life instead of just growing up and then ignoring familial relationships. The fact that women now have their own careers, consequently placing less emphasis on the family and home than in the past, has actually weakened the practice of home education and bonds of familial relationships.

Women have always been the root of culture and society in holding families together, and because this glue has been weakened by the fact that they now work outside their homes, it is even more important to teach children to take care of others while also providing them with positive examples of filial piety to help keep the family system alive. Children should not be brought up thinking that the state is their parent and that they should depend upon the state for everything. This model has never worked in history and is a recipe for total disaster. While modern trends call for us to re-evaluate the issue of the woman's role in society today, which is a large adult educational issue previously given shape by the Han dynasty classic *Lienu Zhuan* (*Biographies of Exemplary Women*) by Liu Xiang, we don't handle this topic at the elementary grades but simply teach the children how to be good people.

In the educational system we must cultivate this idea of *nurturing others*, which is predominant in Chinese culture, otherwise children may develop the tendency to grow up selfish and neglect familial relationships. We can already see that the institution of marriage is threatened because of demands for independence, and thus it is often hard to find stable relationships today because they call for caring sacrifices from both parties. You therefore have to nurture the heart for these ideas to take hold, which is one of our Taihu School's educational objectives. Educational professionals don't normally think about these things since they cannot be measured, but in fact it is precisely this type of emphasis that produces a better world.

Hence, at our school we focus on teaching life skills and the social skills of strong relationship building. We teach the children how to get along in groups, with older individuals, and in paired relationships. We teach them how to take care of one another. They are also taught how to adjust themselves (their minds and bodies) according to various situations, and how to deal with issues such as their bodies, objects, tasks, people and situations. Everything is done with awareness and respect and we teach the children to try to do their tasks with a heart of joyfulness and without complaint.

As they learn how to do things like daily chores, which simply take practice to learn, the children slowly develop confidence that they can master new things in other areas. We never anticipated this benefit to appear from our school, but parents have told us that their children are now not afraid to learn new things or enter into new situations because they just take everything as something new to master. They don't suffer from any extraordinary fears or stress when confronting unfamiliar things because they do this all the time, so it is easy for them to try new things without any fear of failure. This is definitely a positive trait we wish to instill in children as a lifelong habit. Furthermore, since they have been trained to relax and have been shown time and again that they can master anything after some time and consistent effort, they develop a *mindset of problem solving* that we never expected.

At our school we don't actually set out to teach children how to handle stress, but rather our approach has always been to *teach them how to relax*. In using this approach, we have found that stresses then rarely build up. This is a different approach from teaching people how to deal with stress, which is the approach that most adults must turn to, but we have found that this approach avoids most of the problems of stress arising in the first place. This surprising result is similar to the fact that we have found that children actually like to relax their minds and practice meditation. It is the adults who don't like to meditate because they cannot rest their minds, and so they think children don't like to meditate whereas we have actually found that they love it. Acquainting a child with virtuous ways is also a type of meditation because the more familiar one's mind is with virtue, the calmer and more peaceful it becomes.

Previously we mentioned that we found that children can concentrate for long periods of time if you teach them to do so, but researchers think they can only concentrate continually for about 40 minutes. I believe this is because they were just timing the natural tendencies of their attention spans and thinking this is the way things should be, but this is not the way to optimally structure a learning environment. To really learn something you must stay with it to become able to penetrate deeply into the subject matter, and that requires more concentration time than just a 40-minute class session. In fact, you won't even have a full 40 minutes of teaching in a normal class session since some of that time has to be devoted to taking roll, collecting homework and other administrative duties.

In Chinese and Indian culture, concentration is the recognized basis for developing *samadhi* or mental quiet. Concentration is therefore important to learn because it is the basis of self-cultivation. Children love to go deeply into topics and can concentrate on certain activities for hours, but once again it is the adults who lose patience and want to mix things up with more variety. We feel that you should not always be stimulating kids with new things but should let them stay with a topic they like for a long time, and this is a conclusion that our grand teacher and our school has arrived at that perhaps differs from the view commonly accepted in modern educational circles. No one becomes the master of any skill or topic area until they spend a long amount of time in that area and study it with focus and concentration.

Education means teaching people how to live, so we think that teaching children life skills and self-responsibility is very important, as is allowing them to go deeply into topics (and teaching them how to do so). As stated, parents tell us that this approach produces very adaptable, self-reliant and independent children who are confident when they face new situations, and they strongly exhibit those skills when they move onto different schools upon graduation. Teaching them life skills and how to fully comprehend a situation really changes their character and behavior at home.

Most schools only focus on teaching academic subjects, and they measure their teaching success through children's test scores and IQs. They want children to memorize lots of information and get good grades from regurgitating facts. While some memorization and foundational knowledge is essential, our focus is that we actually want them to master skills and learn how to think independently. There are more benefits to learning analytical, critical thinking than we can possibly cite. We don't want them to master memorization for grades and test-taking as much as we want them to learn how to do things in life. Courses and tests are something you complete, whereas life is something you experience, and so we focus on teaching the processing system and skills they will need for living since *a good life is the final objective.* We want them to cultivate their powers of concentration, be able to solve problems, master various skills, and then vigorously apply their knowledge to situations because *this* is what is important in life. Even though we focus on these things, their national academic scores are just as good, if not better than students of the same age.

There is a popular stereotype that a typical Asian school requires long hours of memorization and exhaustive cramming, but we don't believe in these efforts and the pressures they entail. If you just emphasize memorization and test preparation, children will remember things for a short while, such as for an examination, and then will quickly forget the information afterwards. Children never learn to concentrate for more than the shortest of periods with this emphasis, and modern technology is influencing their attention span to become even shorter. With modern technology people can find instant answers, so we must rethink this emphasis on memorizing all sorts of readily found information and the results this emphasis is producing.

While educators think a good school is also one where the average examination scores are at the top of the ratings lists and good students are those who get "A" grades, we must also ask ourselves if this is really so. We think a good school should educate children in a different way, such as helping them to improve their real life capabilities rather than just follow patterns and memorize information. They have to learn how to incorporate what they learn into their life, and perhaps some of our project-based activities can be compared with the idea of "creative play" found in Europe. Of course, children can enjoy traditional play activities at our school as well, and activities such as camping. We think many outdoor activities where they experience nature are often as important to their development as is a strict emphasis on book learning and academia.

School systems the world over are doing children a disservice to their long-term development by emphasizing academics and standardized test preparation over learning how to concentrate or master real subject matter. Due to excessive screen-watching in this internet age, children are certainly growing up with shorter and shorter attention spans. They are not developing the ability to concentrate or apply what they learn, and that's the real problem rather than low test scores that reflect upon how well children can successfully memorize throw-away information. We want them to be able to live the information we teach them, and so we concentrate on very practical things in their foundational basis such as a way of wisdom thinking and subject matter that we hope they will master and utilize for their entire lives.

Because of the widespread use of the internet today, a particular educational problem for children is that they can often get instant answers to a question. They can quickly get a result they want, and therefore don't concentrate any more on the process of learning or thinking. We think this speediness encourages *superficial thinking* and has certain other drawbacks as well. For instance, we have been to schools where there were no children reading books in the school library, yet there were countless students parked in front of computers connected to the internet.

We think the process one goes through in learning is also important to the goal of education, and with internet usage you are simply getting instant answers to questions while largely bypassing certain aspects of the learning process. What happens, for instance, if the internet goes down? Elementary school children who are taught to depend on the internet for instant answers, and who aren't training themselves to think and question the accuracy of such materials, are in danger of developing the habit of not thinking critically about any topic. How can the practice of accepting superficial answers for problems train leaders to think deeply in order to prevent or solve the challenges facing a nation?

The problem with over-relying on the internet is that it doesn't teach you how to think deeply, properly arrive at sound conclusions, or how to use the information you find together with the skills that will help you in life. In using the internet you really don't go through any process of training yourself as regards *critical thinking*. The information you instantly find sits over there and your life experience sits separately somewhere else. All the children use the internet at home where they naturally learn how to surf and find information, and we have not found them to be lacking computer skills because we don't emphasize it at our school. Actually, we have seen great benefits in that our students prefer real activities instead of addictive internet absorption.

We want to prepare our children for the larger objective of being able to navigate through life, and so we don't focus on certain things, such as grades or standardized tests, which no one will even remember. People are going to be evaluating you in life on your character, personality traits, accomplishments and skills in being able to do things, so we focus on these practicalities rather than grades and test scores. We use tests as a diagnostic to see whether children are mastering certain topics, but it's more important in many situations that they master the process of learning rather than get high marks for some subject because this is how they will actually have to meet new situations in the working world of their careers. They will have to be self-learners and figure out the solutions to problems that they never previously encountered in their studies, so mastering the *process of learning* is generally more important than whether you got an A, B or C in an exam.

The habits and skills that children learn in their formative years are some of the most important treasures you can give them, but in regular schooling we have turned away from this emphasis to just stress the memorization of facts (knowledge) and getting good grades.

As previously explained, we also especially emphasize *politeness and courtesy* at our school. We don't just do this because this is a predominant trait of Chinese culture but because it is part of our emphasis on leading children to being good, kind, virtuous people that have a caring concern for others. It is a way of teaching consideration for others that Confucius called "sincerity" and "loving people," Mencius called "kindness," Taoism calls "virtue," and which Buddhism calls "compassion." We focus on teaching respect for others because we have found that this actually produces a much deeper result than stressing superficial courtesy and politeness. This approach tends to foster appreciation and kindness to others, but don't get the idea that we are perfect in these areas. There are many times where we have failed in teaching the very virtues we want children to adopt, but we are always trying to improve our teaching methods and live up to our high ideals.

You have to ask yourself what the worth of our education system would be if, when children grew up, they didn't care about their parents because they lacked kindness, concern and filial piety. Contrary to the wishes of many policymakers, a nation becomes stronger *as the family system becomes stronger*, not weaker. Consider what would happen if children didn't want to take care of their parents when they became sick, or refused to help them in other ways. Compassion, kindness, care and concern for others are virtues which all come from consideration and respect. They are all virtues we want to see in others, especially our parents, spouses, children and friends. Humans often tend to be selfish or self-centered, and so teaching consideration and respect is part of what it means to help children change their behavior.

Another characteristic unique to our school is that we try to teach the children *how to live in tune with the changing seasons of the natural world*, and especially as regards the weather. We hope that this idea spreads across China because this is one of the neglected teachings of Chinese culture even though it has been stressed throughout history. This should be part of training everywhere in the world, and we feel that this should be taken as a form of guidance for the Chinese educational curriculum.

We have the American educational system, the British and European school tradition, and we also have a Chinese educational model which we are trying to develop at our school for the benefit of China and its subsequent generations. We think this emphasis on teaching certain topics in tune with the seasons, whenever possible, should be part of any schooling system, and especially within a Chinese educational system. The American and British educational systems over the last one hundred years have dominated the world, and in veering away from attunement with nature have also somewhat harmed the world and the environment at the same time. We think that a Chinese model, based on harmony with nature rather than blatant exploitation, offers us the greatest hope for the future to counteract much of the damage that has been done to the environment because of errant values or policies promoted in the West.

We are specifically talking about teaching the **twenty-four seasons Chinese calendar system** and how to live in harmony with its indications. This system is based on the solstices and equinoxes, and partitions the year into a total of twenty-four seasons. It sometimes uses agricultural metaphors to explain the cyclical seasons. Some Chinese classics, with Taoist influence, tell us how we should adjust our living for each of these twenty-four seasonal periods. In *The Romance Of The Three Kingdoms*, for instance, there are even stories about how Zhuge Liang used his knowledge of the weather, based on this special Chinese calendar system, in his military strategies. The knowledge of weather trends according to this seasonal calendar has been used throughout history for warfare, but we have elevated its purpose to use it as a cyclical guide to various types of education. The teaching of countless topics can be coordinated to the dates of these seasons rather than just holidays.

Every two weeks we teach the children how they should live according to the new season—how they should change their food and clothing and so on—so they know how to protect themselves and live in harmony with nature. After children stay with us over several years and this cyclical living style becomes a habit, it becomes a big benefit for their individual lives and thus the health of the nation.

We bundle these indications up together with the modern principles of science, health, and personal care to make it a cohesive whole, but the point is that these twenty-four seasons guide some of the topics within our curriculum. During certain seasons, the children change their clothes and eat different foods, and we explain why so that they can learn how to adjust their bodies on their own in life to balance them, prevent sickness, or make them stronger. This is a big educational emphasis at which Chinese culture excels, which is teaching children how to adjust themselves to protect their bodies.

We also teach the children **traditional Chinese medical concepts** at the appropriate times, such as not to wear short pants in an air conditioned room or drink cold liquids (since it can put out stomach fire and produce body dampness, phlegm and then other chronic problems), and of course we teach them the best of Western science on related matters, too, such as avoiding junk food and excessive sugar consumption. Whenever you find a culture or civilization that has a superior approach or better knowledge for a situation, we feel you should adopt it (a concept similar to business "benchmarking"), but as previously emphasized, we think that the underlying overall operating system for life in general should be based on the wisdom approach embodied within the Chinese cultural perspective. Chinese culture is our foundation, and we develop that foundation with the best concepts from other cultures and civilizations. This is our goal, and because our school is so young we are always working on developing our curriculum with this in mind.

We teach the children that according to Chinese medicine, you can easily get sick if you are exposed to cold air or strong drafts. You will immediately catch a cold because of a "wind invasion," or get a headache, or slowly weaken your body so that it later becomes susceptible to influenza. Perhaps not immediately, but this cold wind will go into your body and eventually develop into some type of illness that will manifest when it finally gets an opportunity. Our children go outdoors every day for martial arts exercises and other lessons, so they are taught how to protect themselves in all sorts of weather in accordance with the seasons. However, some schools keep them inside giant air conditioned buildings all day long where the windows are closed and the bad air is re-circulated. This is very bad for their health, and it deprives children of the opportunity of learning how to adjust themselves in the real world as our ancestors have done for thousands of years.

A similar mistake is placing a sheet of glass on a table top to protect the wood. This may look classy, but because the glass is cold that coldness can penetrate into your body when you lean on the table with your arms or elbows. Afterwards that internal cold *chi* can later manifest itself as some sickness. Many Westerners do not believe in such things, such as the fact that sexual excesses can weaken the kidneys, drinking cold liquids can weaken the stomach, or air conditioning can cause headaches, but the wisdom of Chinese medicine offers many time-proven observations like this. Of course the Western nutritional warnings about excessive sugar consumption and eating "clean fats" are just as valuable too.

As another example of practical life lessons, we also teach children that they should not walk without slippers when they get out of bed in the morning, otherwise the cold will enter into their bodies through their feet. In the West, mothers typically teach their children not to go outside with wet hair because they might catch cold. This is the same type of idea, but using the Chinese concepts of the twenty-four calendar seasons we also expand on these sorts of warnings. We teach the children how to live in accordance with the seasons of nature as regards their food, clothing, medicine, personal activities, and so forth. Of course, we also combine this with modern Western scientific findings too, such as not allowing too much sugar in the children's diet. Most of the food they eat is actually grown at our school, and we certainly try to make it is as healthy as possible. We are always trying to combine the best findings from the East and West like this just as we always try to synergistically unite the goals of spirituality with the practical needs for living and human relationships.

Chinese literature has expanded upon these twenty-four seasons and what they mean in many dimensions, such as in the fields of science, literature, astronomy and virtue, and we also try to teach these various correspondences when appropriate and link the regularity of this calendar to our celebration of holiday seasons. In general, we often try to coordinate some of our school activities with this traditional Chinese calendar because we have found this to be highly beneficial. Whenever possible, we use the twenty-four seasons to help guide us in structuring some curriculum topics throughout the year. This is an ongoing process.

Most schools change all the subject matter on a yearly basis, but if the children are exposed to the same type of cultural thinking at deeper and deeper levels every year, and trained to live according to these teachings, think of the impact it will have on their lives after their exposure to multiple repetitions. After staying with us for several years (where they have been through several cycles), it really produces a much deeper impact in terms of life habits than from purely studying information as an academic topic, and the children are really training themselves for a richer life of culture in this way. This is what we set out to do, and so we always try to design our curriculum and courses and the experiences we give the children in this way.

This is truly living Chinese culture, and some day the students will be able to pass on this type of deeper understanding of life and wiser way of living within their own families. This is how we try to set up things in various areas. We are always experimenting with different approaches to get this type of deep result, and while we sometimes aren't successful, it is this type of deep penetration—called "smoking" or "perfuming"—that we try to use to help children absorb positive environmental influences. We want the children to think that *doing things in a certain way is just natural* and not just a topic to study and memorize and then forget the next day. Just as in farming where you cannot force plants to grow, you can only provide the positive conditions for children's growth. Good farmers know what those conditions are while bad farmers do not, and so we give a lot of thought to creating those positive conditions which we call "smoking" or "perfuming" influences. Other schools emphasize grades while we emphasize a broader type of learning.

The last relevant example I can think of to illustrate this point concerns a visit we once made to another international school that we often recommend for our students when they graduate. The teachers at this international school felt that we were too strict regarding children's postures, and believed we overly emphasized it. All throughout this school you could find children sitting in bean bag chairs, slouching at desks and so on while the teachers thought this was appropriate because "they were just children."

Our basic premise is that *the proper posture for sitting, standing and walking is not just essential for health, but for concentration.* We are all much more disciplined when we sit and walk properly. It is easier to concentrate as well, and easier to win the respect of others when we have an erect posture. Don't we all hold ourselves a little straighter when someone with an upright posture walks into the room? Somehow we can all feel the presence of a person who sits erect, and then regard them with greater respect.

Why shouldn't we teach this correct posture to our children when they are young before bad postural habits set in and it becomes too difficult to change them? You certainly cannot deny that a more natural but erect posture is socially beneficial, so shouldn't you teach this in school as a life skill? Many of us certainly adjust our own postures when we are in the presence of others who sit and stand erect, so there are deep principles behind our insistence that a child's posture is important. The *chi* (life force) within your body circulates correctly when your posture is correct, and it is probably because we can somehow then sense someone's internal energy that we thus form a higher opinion of them due to that erectness. Many adults tell us that they wish someone had consistently corrected their posture when they were younger so that they did not form sloppy postural habits, and so that is just another of the many things that we do at our school.

During meetings we tend to regard those present with good postures as the professional, Almost everyone prizes having good postural habits when they are adults. However, if you have not developed good postural habits by the time you are an adult then it is very hard to change matters. Therefore it is best to start young. You cannot say that employment hiring decisions are divorced from first impressions either, and so we do everything possible to make sure children grow up with good postures so that they can make good impressions when meeting other people. If you emphasize having a good posture so that it becomes second nature when children are young, they will naturally maintain that posture into their adult years to reap the benefits.

In short, a proper posture is basic to health, but also has many social benefits. We feel that if children sit properly then they will grow up with a better bone structure than if they are allowed to sit anyway they like.

Furthermore, they will be more productive because of better blood and internal energy circulation, and they will learn better when their spines and heads are erect.

A good posture is beneficial for life in countless ways, so all the chairs at our school were specially selected to help support children's growing bone structures whereas in other schools the administrators just buy any chairs that are cheap and seem functional. The point is we want you to see how we try, by creating a deliberate "perfuming" environment, to create influences that will develop natural habits that children can take with them into life for all their benefits. As often stated, this way of invisibly influencing the children without them necessarily realizing what we are doing is how we have tried to design our school, and is the basis of our idea of creating beneficial "perfuming" or "smoking" educational influences. We are certainly not perfect in any of our attempts, and sometimes fail in our efforts, but we are trying to do our best and are always innovating.

You need a strong support system and repetition to help children form new habits or change old habits, and we try to do this in an invisible or soft way as much as possible so that they absorb the best positive influences from Chinese and Western culture and civilization that will help them for the rest of their lives. In short, we don't do these various things simply to satisfy the school academic curriculum or some government learning mandates, but to really help equip the students with the philosophies and values that will help them with living their lives.

7
SOME OTHER SUBJECT AREAS
AND NATIONAL OBJECTIVES

The **Arts and Music** are very important for young children and can transmit something that you cannot give through any other methods of teaching. Confucius placed a great deal of emphasis on music appreciation because the melodies of music teach harmony and can help you adjust your mind and emotions.

We can see how wise he was because we all know that children are definitely affected by the music they listen to, and it can either calm them down or make them restless and excited. Music can help inspire them or help them reach states of inner harmony, or act as a disturbing pollutant. There is also an old Chinese saying that musical trends can lead to extravagant styles within society, which you can sometimes see within the lives of pop singers today, but this is not what we encourage.

We try to produce a pure environment at our school that doesn't have a lot of influences that would disturb the children by leading them to extremes, but we certainly have them practice stirring motivational or emotional songs where they can release their energies and express themselves voluminously. Children often need strong inspirational music because they have a lot of energy and need some way to express it, so our use of music helps them release and channel their energies in a harmonious way. As an international school we also try to expose them to many different kinds of music.

For the arts we have them engage in drawing and various craft activities where they can use their hands and bodies in getting messy, and in this way we give them a chance to touch, explore, experiment and celebrate their own creativity. Our school is populated with all sorts of objects that the children have created in various arts and craft projects over the years, and you can also find colorful pictures posted on walls, pottery sitting on desks, samples of beautiful calligraphy and other things prominently displayed in our outdoor activities center. This also includes classical poems that they write themselves, which often amaze even our teachers.

Children often need exciting things to do to rally their spirits, but we try to channel their energies during these times so they don't go overboard and lose themselves in excessive extremes. Art and Music help move the emotions, and we can, through these avenues, teach children another thing they can use to adjust their spirits. It is hard to express the positive benefits of Art and Music, but the important point is that they both help children get closer to the good parts of human nature. Music, especially, can be used in a positive way to help you adjust your emotions, and we have the children sing "Om Tara" sound yoga once a week to help them align themselves as a group.

Even when we teach **Science**, we are looking at how to practically tie-in the subject matter to human culture, if possible. If we want children to become more innovative and creative, which is more empowering to the individual, We believe we must borrow from the American teaching method that encourages an inquisitive mind rather than a mind that can simply memorize facts or solve equations. Encouraging a *curious, investigative mind* is a secret key to better scientific education. The Nobel Prize winning physicist, Richard Feynman, often attributed his highly successful science career to his father's influence in encouraging his curiosity as to how and why things were the way they were. His father taught him to ask questions, pursue answers on his own, and helped him experience the pleasure that comes from discovery. Leonardo Da Vinci also became great because he pursued his childhood curiosity about everything, and this is how he became an expert advisor on architecture, anatomy and all sorts of other areas besides painting.

This approach to cultivating curiosity, and do-it-yourself "figure-out-ness," is crucial to producing a future generation of innovators and inventors for a nation. While in Chinese culture we often require the children to memorize loads of information, which leads to our commonly criticized tendency of copycatting rather than innovating, in the field of science we should focus on inventiveness, and do so by encouraging children to ask questions and to investigate matters for themselves. We need to encourage creative inquiry, the urge to question and explore, and the search for alternatives dreamt up by the imagination.

When children are taught to develop an independent and inquisitive mind through methods similar to those used by Feynman's father, I am sure that they will start making great discoveries in the sciences that originate wholly in China, and which in turn can then become the basis of unique new industries and developments which will propel society forward. We are primarily talking about children's education at our school, but a new educational approach to the basic sciences can flourish and rejuvenate the nation's economy so that it is less dependent on foreign technological innovation over time. To do this, China must encourage imagination, curiosity and inventiveness in its children such as by supporting events like the Maker Faire in the U.S. which celebrates arts, crafts, engineering, science projects and the "do-it-yourself" (DIY) mindset. The "do-it-yourself" mindset, such as found at Gever Tulley's Tinkering School, is exactly the type of creative self-reliance we wish children to develop and want to see in the nation as a whole so that it grows stronger, but developing this as a national characteristic takes time and a persistent commitment to a larger vision. To accomplish this, we have to change our educational emphasis from "copy this" and "do not make a mistake" to the idea that "trial and error" is what produces new breakthroughs.

We think that a great science teacher should be a deeply cultivated person rather than just an expert on scientific knowledge and thinking. This type of person is rare, but we especially appreciate Math and Science teachers who have a strong classical literature background because you can find that the ultimate truth of the classics, in what they try to lead people to, is very high stage science. Only a very culturally cultivated teacher can recognize this, and those are typically Math and Science professionals who also have a deep understanding of the classics. This is the type we look for at our school.

For instance, the *I-Ching*, which the children study, always talks about impermanence and change. It denotes the fact that the universe is in a constant state of transformation. This type of understanding is actually very high science as well as philosophy. Since Taoism teaches you how to grab hold of some of these transformations and guide them naturally to get the specific results that you want, it can be said that many of the principles within Taoism naturally tie in with scientific thinking.

The *I-Ching* is an important Chinese classic that most schools fail to teach, and yet many of its passages represent a higher level of understanding of scientific principles along with a unique way of looking at the world to help guide your behavior. In Buddhism, for instance, we are taught that because no thing stays constant, we cannot grasp anything and hold onto it as a constant state of being. When a Science teacher understands such high level cultural teachings and can match them with scientific instruction, this is really one of the abilities we prize at our school.

There are many Chinese classics that lead to higher truths about the world, human nature, and the original energy of the whole universe. The search to find that original energy is actually a major pursuit within modern science, but many of the Chinese classics try to lead us to understanding that ultimate nature through the avenue of investigating the mind. Many classics say that you can find this ultimate energy by tracing the human mind back to its ultimate source, and yet if you never learn how to reach a state of inner calmness so that you can concentrate without distraction, it will be impossible for you to do this. This is why inner quiet and stillness are prized within Chinese culture. At our school we try to teach those skills right from childhood so that they are always available in life for whenever you need them. They are mental skills necessary for accomplishing great things in life, and also for those who want to reach the goal of the Chinese sages in finding that source nature of the individual which is called our true self.

We don't emphasize this type of cultivation at our school, but we certainly give children the foundational skills ("all the pieces") so that they can pursue this type of self-cultivation later in life if they want, just as Confucius recommended. We only provide the foundational skills necessary so that if they want to pursue a higher meaning, as often talked about by the Chinese sages, they have the required preparatory training to do so since it is a natural tie-in to being a virtuous person.

As our grand teacher emphasized, we have taken this as one of the two major purposes of our school because it is one of the central concerns of Chinese culture and civilization. It is even in *The Great Learning*, but everyone today, in the superficial pursuit of wealth, has ignored these types of lessons. This is despite the fact that they are the basis of personal relationships, how people can cultivate themselves to become better human beings, live better lives, and how we can create good fortune for everyone. This is a result that cannot be bought using money.

Let us now explain our thinking on how we try to teach the children **human being skills** through our methods of teaching physical education. Our children exercise everyday through the **martial arts**, rather than simply P.E. (physical education), because the martial arts produce better long-term physical benefits for their growth and for their lives. They can even be used as an entryway into cultivating the Tao (cultivating to reach enlightenment) if they want, though most people don't know this fact.

Children are full of energy and need to develop their bodies through exercise, but what type of exercise is the most appropriate? We want the children to learn how to integrate their bodies and minds, and martial arts are one of the very best ways for doing this since they teach children how to coordinate their energy, mind and bodies all together. You don't normally get this result through teaching calisthenics, team sports or other P.E. activities. Therefore we teach certain types of martial arts that are appropriate for their age and bodies, and this practice is transformative when it is the right kind of practice. As per Nan Huai-chin's guidance, we teach the children Shaolin *kung-fu* and Wudang *kung-fu* rather than *tai chi*. We also teach them *xiao hong qian, xuan gong quan, da hong quan, fu hu quan, wu bu quan,* and *lian huan quan.*

We don't overstress martial arts as do many *kung-fu* academies, but certainly feel that they are more important than sports training or ordinary P.E. activities even though the children also play basketball, soccer and other typical sports at the school. Many *kung-fu* schools teach martial arts without teaching proper breathing methods at the same time, and those children then tend to grow up smaller in stature. This is another reason we don't over-emphasize the martial arts and have very carefully selected the ones we do teach. The children practice on a daily basis, and devote themselves to forty minutes of exercise in the morning and one hour in the afternoon.

Are there other reasons we emphasize the martial arts over other forms of exercise? Later in life you will still need to exercise but you won't be able to safely play football, soccer or baseball when you are fifty or sixty. How many people have already stopped playing team sports by their thirties and forties?

In their senior years, most individuals either end up doing no exercise at all or have to learn gentler new exercises at an age when they are least likely to do so. Even when you are in your thirties or forties you will have usually stopped engaging in aggressive sports and switched to something much safer and more gentle. However, if you go to any Chinese park then you will see seniors still practicing some form of martial arts for exercise that they are also using to adjust their *chi*, mind and spirits. Therefore, with these facts and the long-term view in mind, you should ask yourself what type of exercise should be a foundational basis for children in their schooling. The Western educational system has neglected both wisdom and long-term planning, preparation and consideration in teaching P.E., but we do the exact opposite in the way we train children at our school.

The martial arts can be practiced your entire life *with increasing benefits as you get older*, whereas we cannot say the same for other sports. They can even be used to help you cultivate to "attain the Tao," so why would one want to emphasize other sports instead? We therefore provide teachings on how to practice the martial arts *now*, when the children are young, so that martial arts can then be successfully practiced all their lives. We give children the familiarization with martial arts *now* so that they can keep fit and active well into their senior years. Because of the familiarity with martial arts they gain now, they will not be afraid of them when they get older because they won't be something new but will just be second nature. Thus, they are more likely to practice these exercises as they get older, and will be able to pick them up again in their senior years to help stay healthy. That's a time when adults need to particularly concentrate on maintaining their health.

As stated, the martial arts progression from *wai-going* to *nei-gong* to *Tao-gong* is even one of the traditional Chinese avenues for being able to cultivate seeing one's true nature, so we provide a foundation for that later possibility through many routes at the school, including the forms of martial arts exercise we have selected for the children to practice. Whether the children go on to use this later in life and progress onwards to *nei-gong* and then *Tao-gong* is up to them. We just focus on providing children with an appropriate avenue of exercise that is also simultaneously a life skill and foundation that might make this possible. They are therefore taught the basic exercises that can help them develop their internal energies, which is one of the important contributors to good health and the basis of spiritual development too.

We also teach them how to be good human beings but in doing so we don't stress anything along the lines of religion. However, we do transmit the gems of Chinese culture, which you can definitely say are involved with spirituality because they help us cultivate the human spirit. The contents of the great Chinese classics certainly are entangled with the streams of Buddhism, Taoism and Confucianism that have helped define Chinese civilization. This is a fact that you cannot escape, and the watering of these great rivers has led to the unique development of Chinese culture.

As often stated, in Chinese culture you must consider Buddhism as a department store that contains many things you might use for life, Taoism as a drug store that contains medicines for when you (or the country) are sick, and Confucianism is like a food store that you need to visit everyday. The thoughts and ideas of these great cultural rivers have made their way into the classics that have helped define, elevate and preserve Chinese culture, and our students study these classics.

As you can see, we *take the long view* when teaching exercise to children. The traditional Chinese approach is to apply wisdom to any situation, which means always *thinking long-term*. "Applying wisdom" always means thinking long-term when selecting what to do now. This is why we have the children recite the medical classics, familiarize them with herbs, and introduce them to the idea of self-care and self-adjustment with Chinese medicine, which most people can then practice their entire lives. In this way, by adopting the idea that they are responsible for their own health, they will often take personal actions that can avoid a lifelong dependency on pharmaceutical drugs and doctor's care that can overburden a health system. This is summarized in the Chinese saying, "seven parts to cultivate and three parts to remedy," which means that most of your health problems should be handled by the self-adjustment of living well and taking care of yourself so that only a smaller amount of problems require treatment. Such types of grand planning—to train people how to adjust themselves and that they should handle small health problems on their own rather than immediately run to the doctor—should definitely begin in the childhood years.

We also teach the children and their parents the importance of avoiding excessive amounts of sugar in the diet, which prevents many health problems. We teach them how to adjust their bodies, clothing and activities according to the twenty-four seasons, and so prevent many problems in this way too. As stated, we teach them martial arts practices, which they can practice to keep fit into their senior years, and which can also lay the foundation for them being able to cultivate greater internal energies and calmer mental states. We teach them how to adjust their spirits and emotions through music and sound yoga. We teach them how to calm their minds, avoid stress and relax through meditation and exposure to nature. We try to teach them how to avoid carelessness and reduce accidents through the emphasis on mindfulness and respect in watching their thoughts and what they are doing. We teach all these skills so that they gain some familiarity with how to adjust their bodies and minds.

The Western educational system largely ignores the long-term considerations of health education, and thus many national medical systems are overburdened because countless medical problems arise that could have easily been prevented through proper training and the spirit of self-adjustment. People get sick because they were never taught how to take responsibility for their own health, and were not taught the superior ways of diet and adjustment available that have been developed over the centuries. For instance, Western scientists are just beginning to discover the Chinese teaching for longevity that one should never eat until one is entirely full, but leave the stomach about 20% empty. This certainly helps to avoid obesity and all the related health problems that go with it.

When people are not taught to take responsibility for their health, when they get sick they must lay themselves at the mercy of an expensive and overburdened medical system that they blindly expect will cure them. They become overweight due to wrong diets, develop errant mental tendencies because they cannot relax their minds, and are taught to become dependent on expensive pharmaceuticals rather than try to solve health issues on their own. Which system would you rather build for your nation?

Teaching **Mathematics** is a more difficult topic to discuss than martial arts or health. It is one of the subject areas where we definitely need tests to see whether the children are mastering the subject material. We don't believe in a system totally without tests and grades, because in Mathematics, you need some diagnostic way to determine if the children are mastering both the basic skills and knowledge they will need for life. We therefore use grades as both a benchmark for the school to be able to understand a teacher's level of performance and to understand the children's level of mastery for some topic. But as in the Finnish school system, we use them as a guide rather than as the end purpose of the educational process. We need grades at times, but don't let any emphasis on grades distort the educational process. Let us explain why.

Our students live at our boarding school, so we see all sorts of personalities and develop a good understanding of why certain children behave the way they do. It is just a plain fact of life that some children are lazier than others and don't like to study. Some tend to be naughty as their basic personality too. These two types of children typically don't work hard and therefore they get bad grades because they haven't mastered a topic. Others get bad grades because they don't understand a topic. Those poor grades usually indicate that the children haven't been given enough time yet to master the materials, or the teaching method is unsuitable for them and they need a different way to learn the topic. For those children it is an issue of time or the teaching approach to get them to the level of mastery that we wish for them.

We try to focus on the individual situation of each child when it comes to learning, and we can do this because we live with them 24/7, as parents normally do at home. Thereby we develop a good understanding of their natures. Most schools have designed their education system as an academic treadmill where children are pumped out as if they are finished goods on a production line, but we don't do that. Other schools use grades to categorize children and sort them into different levels with relevant labels. It seems as if the whole system of public education is only focusing on academic scores, rather than true learning, in a protracted system that prepares students for the sole purpose of university entrance. We use grades in a different way. We use the grades as a diagnostic mechanism to see where the children need help in mastering certain types of subject matter. We use them to spot problems such as the children not studying or needing more time in an area. Then we can approach their problem through an individualized solution.

We are interested in the individual's needs because our goal is to provide the basic life skills and foundation that each one will require in life. We want to absolutely make sure every child masters the basic topics and develops the skills, knowledge and understanding they need. This is why we give lots of extra help to slow children and naughty children. For instance, our punishment for naughty children who don't want to study, which turns out to be an incredible motivator, consists of not letting them (as well as the lazy children who don't want to study) participate in Friday outdoor classes with everyone else. Also, they might not be permitted to join the daily meditation class and must recite the classics instead as a form of discipline.

In cases of children with great disciplinary faults who are just too unruly because they fail to respond to all our efforts, we have no other choice than to suspend them from the school. Sometimes this type of suspension is the only way to save a child because it provides a wake-up call to both the child and parents that the problem is serious and the child's behavior needs to be amended to prevent greater problems in life.

In the **Meditation class** the children basically have quiet time where they can sleep, relax, or meditate and the choice is totally up to them. We call it the "meditation class" but there is no particular focus on meditation but just quiet time, which is a period of calmness and relaxation. If they are naughty or bad, one of the "punishments" is that they have to recite the classics rather than enjoy this quiet time, and you would be surprised how much they want to enjoy that quiet time rather than do something else. As to the slow children who aren't mastering a topic, we just give them lots of individual time and attention on those topics.

Our philosophy with **Mathematics** is that it is a topic that requires you to master both skills and knowledge. There are certainly some mathematical things to memorize, like multiplication tables, although in the best of worlds we also want the children to learn how to do calculations in their head, or how to use an abacus. We want them to develop a physical feeling for some mathematical concepts, and skills such as measuring things, but are still looking for the best methods to teach certain topics such as quantitative reasoning. We think there has been a struggle in teaching Mathematics throughout the centuries in every culture, which is why people tend to hate Math since no one has yet come up with a perfect teaching method.

For instance, fractions and proportions are important in daily life. You certainly need to develop a feel for fractions and a proficiency in using them because you will have to handle them constantly. Many people will find jobs where they are dealing with bank interest rates, profit margins, growth rates, probabilities, etc. and so we want to give the children a physical feel for this sort of thing. Our children only go up to grade six, so we don't have to worry about high school topics like calculus, but since we're on this topic I want to point out that educational systems should probably emphasize statistics over calculus since this is a far more valuable topic to the average person in life. Statistics is a topic that they will use in the real world whereas we cannot say the same for calculus. This emphasis on calculus as the summit of mathematical training, rather than statistics, is something that we should consider changing in the educational system for teenagers.

Almost everyone will be dealing with statistical concerns on a daily basis in many facets of life, and hardly anyone will be dealing with calculus unless they are going to become an economist, engineer or scientist, so we should rethink this issue of emphasizing calculus over statistics in the upper grades. Educational systems the world over teach algebra, geometry, trigonometry and calculus but you find that the graduates of the advanced grades know little about practical things like compound interest, risks, uncertainty, randomness and other mathematical matters which they have to deal with everyday in personal finance. This is strange, especially as most parents want their children to become wealthy, but we don't even stress the relevant mechanical skills that will help people manage their money.

Other than emphasizing statistics, another subject we might consider introducing into a national curriculum for the higher grades is the topic of **curiosity, creativity, innovation and inventiveness**. The method of

TRIZ, invented by the Russian Genrich Altshuller after studying hundreds of thousands of patent inventions, provides an interesting framework for teaching inventiveness. If we teach some of these ideas, rearranged in the right way, to teenagers who love to experiment and who have access to 3D printing and electronic or mechanical components, then they will certainly experiment to create new things. Many young adults in their teen years know few barriers to creativity and love to mechanically experiment to build new things. The projects which some of them complete with computers often put to shame the efforts of college educated adults who are employed full time. If you offer them opportunities you will find them and then can encourage them.

Some of these teenagers are the potential new inventive geniuses of our time who don't need to wait until college to get started at innovation, but due to lack of foresight we rarely give them a vehicle to help them learn the practicalities of invention such as how to create prototypes for what they can envision as is now available with 3D printing software. There is a better way, and there is a reason we are mentioning this. While the explanation may seem a bit technical, this is important material that national educators, policymakers and strategists all over the world must understand at the highest levels if they are truly concerned with the long-term prosperity of their nations.

The basis of national prosperity in all countries over the last few hundreds of years has shifted away from agriculture to manufacturing. Even though we run special gardening/farming projects at our school in conjunction with a national university to educate children on the importance of agriculture (we want to educate children about growing food, which is the basis of their health, and the problems of diet-related diseases), the basis for a large country to grow more prosperous is no longer simple commodity exports such as food, timber and minerals, whose prices you cannot control because of a world marketplace, and it isn't due to service-based industries either. The key to prosperity is always "increasing returns to scale" activities that command monopolistic prices, offer chances for innovation, and which can generate high wages. Manufacturing has always fit this bill, and there are many reasons why history clearly shows that a country that turns to manufacturing becomes rich, but loses its wealth and standing once it loses its industrial manufacturing sector.

While the theory sounds seductive that "information industries" are the future of wealth production, even a "knowledge-based" economy has limits to its potential prosperity. You cannot create wealth simply by printing money, or by a financial sector either. Unfortunately, if you sell natural resources or commodities to make money, they are subject to world market prices you cannot control because of competition, while their output follows the natural laws of "decreasing returns to scale." This means that it always costs more to produce that one extra marginal barrel of oil, ton of copper or extra acre of corn. Manufacturing, however, gives you the chance of earning increasing profit margins whenever you produce more. Those increasing margins, which are the results of lower costs derived from a learning curve, when coupled with increasing sales demand, together produce wealth for an individual or nation over time. In other words, if you produce more of an innovative product that has increasing demand, and your margins keep getting better over time, these two factors will help you grow rich. Manufacturing is the key industry within a nation that offers this capability, but it requires innovation-based training.

Studies therefore have shown that a country lives or dies, and becomes a leader of the world or a follower, due to the level of its manufacturing exports. If you don't make something that the world wants, which will also result in a trade surplus rather than a deficit, then you will not produce this advantage for your economy that is the basis of prosperity and national employment. You must keep producing and then exporting innovative things that the world wants for your country to become richer. A debt-based economy promoting consumption that does not produce goods itself cannot maintain prosperity over the long run whereas an inventive and innovative manufacturing economy can. It will keep more people employed as well.

The question then becomes how to create this economy? You must create *unique, innovative items* that the world wants rather than be a non-innovative copycat manufacturer who has lower margins. To become a world leader, a country must therefore develop its own technology rather than continually import technology and innovation from elsewhere, and it therefore needs to create an educational system that *produces innovative thinkers and creators*. It needs a schooling system that encourages people to make discoveries in the basic sciences while also championing creativity, technology, innovation, and invention. It needs to cultivate a certain **do-it-yourself mentality** of curiosity, creative inquiry, exploration and innovation. Unfortunately, there is no "silver bullet" or cookie cutter recipe for accomplishing this.

How can you cultivate a new national ability for creativity and innovation rather than just buy technology from other countries, or copy dead-end low margin industries that might pollute the nation? You must teach people how to become the inventors of new things, which in turn require manufacturing to be produced. The production of unique products with growing demand produces riches for a country, but to have this you must first develop a national characteristic of creativity and innovation, rather than mimicry, so that these new products are actually invented.

Designing unique products starts with creativity and inventiveness, which is a style of thinking we typically leave to college training, but you can in fact start teaching creativity in high school when children are most likely to experiment on their own to build new things. You simply need to expose the children to the right ideas and guiding principles, such as books that reveal how the mechanical innards of various inventions are constructed, and also give them the right tools and materials (such as software or component modules that can be easily assembled) so that they can play with them and test their dreams. You don't have to give them any special trade school training but just let them tinker, and because of the inventive spirit they will usually figure things out.

A country like China that wishes to become stronger, wealthier and less dependent on foreign innovation must think long-term and focus on that first step of the wealth generation process. It must support the development of inventive minds through a style of education that encourages hands-on experimentation and a can-do attitude, but no country has a grand strategy to do so. One way is to interest teenagers in building new things by giving them the means to do so, and then they will often take those skills and create new products and industries as they grow older since they already love doing it.

A relevant story comes to mind about how the famous hi-tech publisher, Wayne Green, helped the King of Jordan solve Jordan's problem of having to bring expensive technicians in from all over Europe to maintain its telephone systems and radio communications. Green told him to put ham radio clubs in the schools and youth clubs so that the children would have fun learning about electronics, and to hire an instructor to go from school to school to teach children basic electronics. The cost was minimal. The Prime Minister, military leaders and other officials loved the idea. Three years later Green was invited to Jordan to see what had been accomplished. Just from this tiny emphasis alone, because higher officials had developed a unified spirit and applied themselves to solving the problem in an indirect but wise way, Jordan had become more advanced in hi-tech than any other Arab country. It was all due to this simple, low cost method of promoting a relevant training avenue while making it fun and interesting for children to unleash their talents and energies in this manner. This same type of approach can certainly be used in different ways to foster more creativity, inventiveness and innovation within a nation. Chinese history offers many examples of how rulers have fostered internal grand strategies in this way, and they all started because the ruler and his ministers recognized a future need and then became committed to producing results through natural means, just as we see in the story of Wayne Green. The Chinese sage Kuan Tzu, in particular, teaches you how to bring about the results you want naturally without too much structure or effort. Instituting too much structure in order to try and produce a specific end result can actually be deadly poison to the outcome you hope to achieve.

Many people know that an American named William Edwards Deming revolutionized Japanese industry by teaching a very simple concept that Japanese industry subsequently adopted everywhere, which was the idea of instituting quality control in manufacturing processes. The adoption of this very simple but key idea became the linchpin of its march toward national prosperity. Its adoption catapulted the country to a level of wealth and standing previously unknown because no other country chose to adopt that emphasis, which just shows that such a dramatic result can come from simple means. When manufacturing elsewhere finally caught up to the quality offered by Japan, then the country lost its prior advantages, though poor financial policies by the banking industry and government sector also caused Japan to falter. However, it was due to a unification of minds in *applying a simple strategy everywhere* that brought Japan to its pinnacle of power.

If the Chinese wish to become pre-eminent, we must think about addressing the initial step prior to manufacturing prosperity, which is to foster the inventive spirit so as to eventually free the country from a dependence on foreign innovation. We must stress curiosity and creativity rather than just mimicry in our schools, and eventually teach people how to invent things that the world will want. We don't have to leave this task to the late stages of college where we train students to become engineers, but can start preparing for this in high school or even earlier.

The task of producing this type of national result requires a commitment to more research in the basic sciences, but also requires that we foster a type of innovative, creative thinking in our earlier educational curricula. There is a need to teach children how to think and explore in creative ways, just as Taoism tries to teach certain ways of thinking in order to stay healthy or deal with certain situations. You must also encourage curiosity and questioning rather than just the following of orders and instructions. You also have to design your school system in certain ways. For instance, in Finland, which is often recognized as having one of the best educational systems in the world, science classes are capped at sixteen students so that they can perform practical experiments in every class. This is an example of the right type of thinking, which is to structure the school system with the result you want to produce in mind. The Finnish policymakers re-designed Finland's education system after they sat down and determined what skills the country would need to compete in the changing world economy. The result is the world class schooling system they have today which was designed with specific purposes in mind.

Many children love to experiment and build things because they have a special intelligence in this area. For those who do, you should give them this opportunity when they are young so that they can foster these skills and interests. For instance, studies clearly show that if you give teenagers the right tools and materials and show them how to build certain things, they certainly will, and then they will incrementally improve them. They *want* to engage in this type of creativity if you give them the chance.

The nation that cultivates this type of educational approach will gradually but surely produce the next generation of world inventors, and then manufacturers, who will in turn eventually enrich their economies in countless unexpected ways. Achieving this type of goal requires a commitment to long-term strategic planning rather than just hoping things will happen, such as what India committed itself to when developing its Institutes of Technology system, which now rivals or even eclipses MIT in excellence because of that effort.

Since national wealth and prosperity in the long-run will depend on this type of outcome, fostering the mindset of inventiveness and creativity in the education system is part of a grand strategy, like emphasizing statistics over calculus or teaching martial arts and Chinese medicine, which we wished to take this opportunity to mention even though it really applies to the higher grades that we don't teach at our school. Our Taihu Great Learning Center is committed to helping China in as many ways as possible, especially culturally, which is why we have offered some of these ideas to policymakers whose job it is to apply their own deep talents and wisdom to such issues. All countries face challenges along these lines, so they should consider this discussion appropriately.

Governments must always think of first principles and how they wish to benefit their countries when they develop their educational systems. They should think about putting into effect wise strategies that *over the long run* will achieve their goals, such as helping citizens attain good livelihoods with rising incomes so that they are not impoverished and become destitute wards of the state. If they make the right decisions to do the best thing in every area, even when it initially costs more money, the ideal outcome is the potential for China to eventually become as respected as it was during the Tang dynasty when people from all over the world came to learn from it as the cultural leader of Asia and most advanced nation in countless fields. The stakes are high in a world of global competition, where every nation wants to stay at the forefront of developments, so we need to really think about whether we would like this to happen.

We can bring about such a result if we abandon the practice of solely considering financial profits and costs when making policy decisions, which often causes us to mistakenly forget humanistic principles and do *what is wrong* simply because it costs less or will make more money. Principles, rather than profits, need to guide decisions. We need to take wisdom, virtue and deep cultural thinking on what constitutes "improvement" as our guides to policy decision-making so that we can do *what is right* rather than what is merely profitable. As Nan Huai-chin stated, the big challenge confronting us is how to unite and harmonize the cultures of materialism and spirituality, which includes the concepts of virtue, contributive behavior and self-cultivation.

As Mencius warned the King of Liang, if mere profit-seeking thinking gains control over a nation, those above and below will soon all be trying to profit at the expense of one another, and the state will eventually be imperiled. Some say we can see Mencius' warning in the economic state of America and the European Union today. Sages stated that if profit is put ahead of righteousness and precedence is not given to humanity and justice, disorder will soon follow. The Grand Historian also said, "Whether it is found among the upper or lower classes, the degeneracy due to the lust for profits is basically the same. When those in public office profit unfairly, then the law will fall into a state of disorder. When those in the private sector profit by deception, then business will fall into a state of disorder. When business becomes disorderly, people will become combative and dissatisfied. When the law becomes disorderly, a nation's citizens will become resentful and disobedient. This is how people get to be so rebellious and belligerent that they don't care if they die." These are prescient words for the civil unrest we often see in the world.

Misshapen thought at the leadership helm can threaten to destroy the social order and prosperity of the nation, which is why we emphasize *virtue and deep cultural values* as the inner guides for behavior at our school. It sometimes costs more to do the right thing in society, but many things should not be permitted in society regardless of the monetary benefits they might bring. Only by taking the "virtue of the situation" into account, rather than focusing solely on the profitable potential of money-making, can we then arrive at proper decision-making standards that will prevent us from harming or even destroying ourselves over the long run.

This is so obvious, but few people take the approach that Nan Huai-chin taught, to see the bigger issues and emphasize the key principles or areas that will impact future development and bring about benevolent results for all the parties involved. For instance, many years ago the President of a northern Chinese university visited him asking what it could do to help the Chinese educational system. Russia at that time was breaking apart and lacked funds for its educational institutions while China was growing richer, and he immediately responded that the Chinese universities should hire the Russian university professors and scientists who now had no jobs or incomes. This win-win strategy would immediately help the Russians while bringing their advanced knowledge and skills to China to help build the nation. Throughout my many years with him, he was constantly offering advice in many fields along such lines, and was absolutely committed to the ethical development of China. He taught us that everyone should be devoted to strengthening their national culture and assisting their nation whenever possible.

Our goal at the Taihu School is not only to help prepare children for life, but to also in this way contribute to the nation and slowly make the country stronger. Is this not a goal of the educational system? We are always trying to do this in various ways other than just educating children, and sigh at our own shortcomings when we remember the vows of the Confucian Chang Tsai (Zhang Zai) "to establish true mind for the universe, establish direction for humanity, re-establish the discontinued studies of the ancient sages, and establish great peace for ten thousand generations."

A school cannot get away from the three fundamental educational goals of trying to produce good people, good citizens and prepare students so that they can make their own independent ways in the world with good livelihoods. These things will make a nation stronger rather than weaker, and require that we prepare children for the *real world* rather than concentrate on the paper world of standardized tests and exams that kills creativity and academically produces "look-alike children." We want to celebrate diversity. We want children to grow up to be lifelong learners who can critically think for themselves and become leaders who can solve problems and create new beneficial possibilities for society rather than just unthinking, obedient followers of uniformity and conformity. How will a country's citizens find happiness in life if they are taught this is all there is? The future needs more creative innovators, entrepreneurs and developers rather than people trained to fit a particular mould. It needs leaders with a moral conscience who will make wiser decisions that take into account ethical principles of what is right and wrong. Everyone can see that the Western educational system has been veering away from these directions to its own detriment, so we must all be careful not to open ourselves up to the eventual forces of deterioration and decay and repeat any relevant mistakes that we might see elsewhere.

For **History**, our method is to teach historical stories of great events and the biographies of great heroes, who often stand as models of positive virtues the children might emulate. Giving children role models they might emulate is one of the best ways to instill within them a sense of character and virtue.

Many schools want children to memorize lots of historical names, places and dates, but later in life most people forget them. You definitely want children to know a core set of material, but we must also remember that most people today can easily look things up. The more important thing in this age of knowledge-technology is to know where and how to get knowledge when you need it, and how to organize this into definite plans of action. We should therefore rethink this heavy emphasis on cramming and memorization (or at least should teach *"super memory" methods* in the classroom) and perhaps emphasize the development of other traits that will better serve individuals for life. What is more important than memorizing dates, for instance, is to *derive lessons from history* (such as strategies), as emphasized in many Jewish Biblical curricula, and introduce the children to historical individuals they might choose to admire as *role models*.

One of the important things about history is that it does not necessarily repeat itself, but events often do rhyme (look similar to one another). If you don't study history to absorb its lessons of what works or doesn't work, then you can certainly repeat those very same mistakes. History enables us to see the difference between the actual and intended consequences of ideas, so studying history is a way to teach deep thinking. Whenever you teach children to think about the consequences of their actions, in a way you are fostering veneration for historical lessons-type thinking.

Thus, we place a particular emphasis on extracting the lessons of history for our children, and our model encourages them to think along those lines by trying to extract the lessons of the classics and bring them into their own lives. One of the special traits of Chinese culture is to derive general lessons or tendencies from the study of a larger set of facts or body of knowledge, and then present them in a useful form of "wisdom lessons" that one can use for life. Chinese culture excels in deriving strategies or policy lessons from history, as seen in works like *The Three Strategies of Huang Shi Gong*, the

Sixteen Strategies of Zhuge Liang, the *Thirty-Six Stratagems,* and *Records of the Grand Historian* by Sima Qian. The Asiapac publishing series of cartoonist Chih Tsai Chung, even though they are comic books, does a wonderful job of making these types of lessons available to both children and adults.

In the Western educational system, the emphasis is to discover the discrete facts or exact principles that rule situations, and while this works for the fields of science and mathematics it doesn't always work for the humanities. The Western educational emphasis is becoming increasingly focused on the natural sciences while relegating the exploration of humanist thought as a waste of time even though it is the basis of human culture. Historical thinking is therefore not prized for this and many other reasons. However, it is extremely valuable. Just as we teach our students to think about the outcome of unintended consequences because they lacked respect for whatever they were doing during some activity, this type of behavioral analysis can be tied into how they look at history.

In short, the approach we take at this young age is to teach the stories of history, and to try to derive lessons from history and the classics so that the children discover a deeper meaning that touches their lives, as opposed to just memorizing facts that they would soon forget. This is what is important because the principles and lessons of history are something you should use to solve problems and make better decisions in life, especially if you are a policy maker for your country. Chinese culture excels at examining history to derive various principles and lessons for guidance, so we emphasize this wisdom aspect of our culture when teaching the children.

8
TEACHERS AT SCHOOL AND AT HOME

The last topic we should discuss is our teachers and parents, and the relationship between the two at our school. When we first started the Taihu School, one of the attributes We were searching for when hiring teachers was kindness. In addition, we always asked, "If my child grows up to be like him or her, would I be happy?" That was another of the most important questions I asked when evaluating potential teachers because I knew that the children would copy some of their behaviors. Teachers are role models who teach character by example, and so I wanted the children to see virtuous behavior in the reality they perceived, otherwise it would not take root. Ordinary schools just hire teachers to teach academic subjects, but I wanted to have teachers who were also exceptional humanistic role models for the school, who would make a great impression on the children.

The teacher is a role model for students because the children will often copy their behavior just as they will observe, mimic and then copy the behavior of their parents, siblings, relatives, and friends. We therefore place a big emphasis on finding teachers that represent good role models for children because of their personalities and ways of doing things. The way they talk, walk, treat others, and even dress are all factored into our selection process because our emphasis is on training the children to be good people, to fit in with society, to develop harmonious social skills, and be effective in the world with good habits and behaviors.

If the educational emphasis is just on having children "getting smarter" by acquiring knowledge but neglects the other practical aspects of being a virtuous human being, how will we create the future leaders who can save the nation in times of difficulty? Are they born from just intelligence? Mencius's mother, who admirably moved three times before she found a place suitable for his upbringing, showed that *we must be very careful about the surrounding environment and other influences we expose children to when they are young* because those influences will affect their development. Thus it is very important for you to pick a school teaching the right topics and values system, having the right sorts of teachers, and offering positive environmental influences. Our goal is to teach the foundational skills that will produce a nation of both virtuous *and* talented individuals. Accomplishing this depends on selecting teachers not just for their training skills, but because they represent good role models.

Today, as long as they have the required subject skills, we typically give teachers two months to prove their effectiveness in teaching and their ability to influence children to develop in a positive fashion. We are not just looking for someone who knows their subject material, but want to see how the teacher will get along with the children in terms of being a positive role model for their personal development. After two months of working with them, we will know a teacher quite well and the influences they are producing. That is when our senior staff decides if we should keep them or not.

One of the reasons we have higher teacher turnover at our school is because our standards for teachers are so high. They have this responsibility of being excellent at teaching, being good role models, and being committed to helping children transform themselves. If we are not getting the role model we want for our students, we would rather let a new teacher go. Then again, because many teachers have heard about our school and what we are trying to do, we also get applicants that are truly committed to these same goals even though we are located some distance from a major city. This is why we are developing a one year **Teacher Training Program** so that they can come, learn and then take some of our methods elsewhere when they leave.

Another requirement for our teachers is that we don't want anyone who will kill the children's imagination or enthusiasm for certain topics. There are extremely successful people with careers in many different fields, and which looked at hundreds of characteristics to see if there was a common denominator to both their outstanding success and happiness. The only commonality, after checking thousands of famous superstars for any common characteristics, was that the parents never put them down or killed their enthusiasm when they were young children. They never called them stupid, or said they couldn't do certain things when they grew up, such as become an astronaut or dancer or whatever. They never yelled at them or criticized them saying they could not handle some task but simply encouraged their dreams. They didn't criticize them for failures but applauded them for trying and encouraged them to reach for the stars and follow their interests. Today you might call this encouraging "self-esteem" but we think the idea is different. Basically, we don't ever want any teacher killing a child's imagination and thus their creativity potential.

When children are very young, whatever they say about their dreams in life doesn't really matter. Next month the ideas you heard today will be replaced by something else, so you should not criticize a child when they are young and mentally role playing different careers or accomplishments, testing different skill sets and trying to find themselves. You should not constantly throw water on their dreams when they say they want to do this or that but should just say to them, "Of course you can do whatever you want or become whatever you want." Naturally, you must immediately correct them, however, if what you hear as a goal isn't something virtuous.

You must also always be careful what you say to young children and how you say it. By stomping on innocent dreams with ridicule and derision, you might create scars on their psyche that will forever dam up their enthusiasm and thus their later attempts to reach for the stars. We actually need more children with positive dreams of the future rather than just conformists who follow he orders of others. If you kill their dreams and enthusiasm, you take away the future potential of the children to achieve whatever they came into this world to achieve. You squash their possibilities for finding their life's calling and experiencing great happiness, success, growth and greatness.

This is why we make a special effort to give our students a safe place where they can try out their own unique talents, natural capacities and skills that they bring with them into this world. You never know if those skills or interests will become the basis of a career or occupation later in life or just remain a temporary hobby or pastime, so we try to expose them to many different types of activities requiring many different types of capabilities. We try to give children the room to explore these inborn talents and test their dreams because these interests are often the seeds of greatness.

We leave it to fate to see where talents and interests will lead but we don't try to kill off any positive imaginations. Many of us can look back to our youth and remember a time we were crushed through some criticism of our hopes and dreams, so we try to make it safe for the children to try many new things with a spirit of exploration. Having the right type of supportive teachers who don't kill off imagination is very important in this way.

If a teacher also has an arrogant attitude of self-importance with students, such as "I am the greatest because I know this topic" or "I am imparting knowledge to you," we also consider this a negative characteristic. We don't want teachers who simply dump data on the children rather than help the children really delve into a topic so they can learn it by experience. We have found that the first type of teacher cannot truly gain the children's respect. A teacher's behavior is what gains children's respect rather than their knowledge, so that's what we emphasize in addition to the fact that every school wants teachers who know their topic well and can teach it.

Our school is run very differently from others because of many issues like this that emphasize the humanities first and foremost, and the many positive stories from parents keep telling us that our environment is special and our strategies are working. We commonly hear that our methodology has helped their children become better human beings and natural leaders when they go to new schools upon graduation. Their personalities, and many disciplinary problems they once had, changed for the better because of the school's special influence. However, it is hard to communicate the sort of successes we typically achieve because every child is different.

Our grand teacher, Nan Huai-chin, often said that what our teachers are doing entailed unimaginably great merit because it has helped many children change themselves in a deep way, and that positive influence will run for many lives. I must truly thank our teachers for being committed to this great task, and for dedicating their lives to children's education. To truly understand what happens, however, you should not listen to us but should talk to our parents to confirm the outcomes they have been telling us. Only in time will we see the long-term result of the special foundation we try to give the children for their lives.

If you therefore ask us how our students are different from children who graduate from other schools, we can only tell you what our parents report back to us. They consistently say that the behavior of their children has improved tremendously, which even their adult friends notice, and that they have adopted all sorts of beneficial habits that also help the family. They seem different from children educated in the ordinary school system in these commonly cited ways:

- They are more confident than other children because they have been trained to solve problems and manage things entirely on their own. They develop a lot of self-confidence because they have been taught to do things they are capable of doing, and this training in self-responsibility tends to make them very self-reliant. They also develop the right attitude about any work they must do.
- They are not afraid to try something new, take risks, fail or be out of their "comfort zone" because they have been taught to take on challenges and "try first" rather than shy away from new situations, and to "never give up." They are also taught "it is never too late for change." Thus, they can more easily adjust to changes and face stresses better than others because they have been trained how to relax. They know that it is okay to fail or make mistakes, and that things don't always work out the first time, so you must be resilient and persistent to simply keep trying until you get things right.
- They have more practical life skills such as table manners and the ability to do housework, greet other people, readily speak to or perform in front of groups, and so forth.
- They also are better than other children in being able to naturally manage their time and schedule personal activities. For instance, they know when they must eat and when they can play, so they design the completion of their tasks accordingly. Parents say they know how to finish their homework ahead of time without needing to be constantly pushed. They have a natural sense of self-direction.

- They tend to be more curious, tolerant and more open-minded than others. Because of having had fewer boundaries, they tend to think independently and creatively. They have been taught it is okay to ask questions rather than remain silent, and instead of memorization have been trained to research for answers and think about the meaning of things. We have tried to help them become self-learners who know how to research and learn by themselves rather than have to wait for others to teach them, and this seems to be working. They have also been trained to accept many different types of people, activities and circumstances so they aren't so rigid in either their internal mental outlook or in their external approach to situations.

- We are told they also become natural leaders when they go to other schools. Whereas other children only know how to study, they actually know how to do many things from personal experience, so they usually become group leaders and often the "best classroom helper" for their new teachers.

- Many of their errant behavioral tendencies often diminish due to the school's educational influence, and so they show great positive behavioral change. The children are taught what it means, from the classics, to cultivate virtue and to be a good human being. We tell them to speak positively and to be polite and kind to others. Perhaps because of our emphasis on respect and getting along in groups, they tend to be more cooperative than other children and have better social skills. They are also less materialistic and tend to appreciate whatever they have as opposed to constantly wishing for more.

- They learn to be mindful by being taught to do everything with respect, and thus learn some degree of focus and concentration, mindfulness and awareness. They have been trained to concentrate on whatever they are doing in hopes of learning how to bring their skills and knowledge together when facing situations. They basically know how to practice mindfulness or introspection, which helps them in terms of focus and self-control.

- They seem more concerned about other people, including parents, grandparents and their friends. For example, they naturally bring tea for guests, and immediately know how to communicate with people on topics they know that the other party is interested in. Part of the reason for this is because they are trained to take care of one another through their senior-junior ("sifu-tudi" older-younger teacher-pupil) relationships.

Thus they don't exhibit many of the single-child problems plaguing society since they have been taught to take care of one another, and thus they have greater cooperative and social skills because of the "shr-tu" relationship that we developed at our school. Because they live in groups and are taught to help one another and share, they tend to be less selfish and more concerned about others.

- They are very conversational because, being in a boarding school, they treat the teachers like parents and so have been taught that they can freely share their thoughts and talk about many things. They learn how to pick up on what you are interested in and naturally turn it into a conversation, so are not shy and inhibited in dealing with other people.

- They are concerned about conservation and the natural environment, and you will find them picking up trash from the ground or telling their parents "let's walk" for a short trip rather than use the car since they know it pollutes the environment. They also love nature because of all the outdoor activities they do everyday. They love camping, eating outside and playing in the grass, and are not afraid of dirt, bugs or sitting on the ground.

- They know how to use various types of Chinese medicine and physical adjustment. For instance, they know what acupuncture points to press when someone is car sick, or what to do in cases of fever. Sometimes they will give their parents massage for certain health conditions, and the parents unsurprisingly report back to us that Chinese medicine works.

- The children also know how to adjust their bodies in other ways such as through diet, clothing, meditation, breathing, martial arts exercise, or sound yoga.

- They can more readily see things from other points of view and know how to easily step into another person's shoes to see their side of a situation. Thus, they can develop a larger view of any situation and come up with solutions that are more stable in satisfying many parties.

As often mentioned, much of what we do in style and execution has been influenced by our grand teacher, Nan Huai-chin, and we take it as part of our mission at the Taihu School and our Great Learning Center to help keep his positive influences alive for society. His own educational philosophy has provided the foundational guidance on what and how we should be teaching. He always said that a big educational emphasis should be on teaching children how to change their behavior for the better whereas the regular educational emphasis just focuses on teaching academic topics rather than helping the children to become better human beings.

Because of genes, their environment and other influences, everyone comes into this world with different skills and personality traits. He said that if you don't learn how to change your negative personality traits, but just learn how to fertilize and further develop what you already have, you can still become a *monster* in life or a great burden on others. Many failures in life are the victims of their own mental defects that they never worked at transforming. Therefore one of the roles of education should be on helping you change any errant or bad personality traits to good ones, and to teach you to think about what "represents virtue" for any situation. In other words, to think about *what is right* rather than what is simply profitable, pragmatic, or efficient. We must switch from allowing a politics of money to rule us, which will certainly destroy us in the long run, and replace that emphasis with a *politics of principles* once again.

All of the Chinese classics on cultivating virtue and goodness are actually about transforming what is bad about our personalities and behavior, so we follow these ideas and try to help guide the children along better lines when we find faults or personality issues that might hurt them (or others) later in life. We also try to give them the skills that they absolutely need in life (that no one else teaches), and naturally we teach all the normal subject matter that you would find in regular schools since they also need this of course. Everyone needs to learn how to read and write, do math and think logically but we especially focus on teaching the children how to draw on themselves for managing their personal situation, whatever it may be, and to use the Chinese wisdom view as their operating or mental processing system. This is why our school is known for "life training."

For instance, when your body is uncomfortable then you can adjust it through exercise and diet, or through breathing, or by medicine, and we teach all these things to the children so that they remember all these avenues and have all these skills available for life. What we are proud of is that these skills are becoming second nature so that the students can access them all life long, but it is up to them to develop these skills further after we give them a working foundation. We don't explicitly teach them anything that constitutes religion, but simply give them a non-denominational foundation for spiritual self-cultivation so that they can pursue this if they choose to do so later in life through many of the roads available in Chinese culture.

For instance, you can adjust your emotions and bodily feelings when they are troubled through music, exercise, art and human relationships. You can also change your behavior by practicing respect, watching your mind with introspection, and by first considering the consequences of your actions before you do anything, or by considering all the trouble and effort and consideration that went into creating the bounty you presently enjoy. You can cultivate your mind to a state of clarity by practicing meditation and concentration. There are many things like this that we could talk about deeply, but here we are just giving a short introduction to some of the principles within our educational philosophy.

Our style exposes the children to very broad influences, but we also focus on individual children and their problems. Therefore our approach is very different from ordinary schools that treat children like little uniform grade machines in a factory, rather than as individuals with unique personalities and special talents. Because our approach is different from the typical educational emphasis, *we require parents to understand what we are doing* so that they can cooperate with us and continue with this educational style via pertinent lessons at home.

As mentioned before, once or twice a year we hold mandatory training weekends for the parents, who actually tell us that they look forward to these sessions because it gives them an opportunity in today's busy world to take a break and spend some time cultivating themselves too. It is great to hear adults with busy schedules say "thank you" simply because you gave them three days of rest where they didn't have to constantly monitor their cell phone or look at their computer. It seems that everyone desires to learn the mental peacefulness skills that we try to teach the children as a natural ability.

Everyone wants a chance to cultivate, but we rarely take the time to do so in life unless we are actually forced to make that initiative. Our Parents Training weekends give the parents that opportunity, and many say they also take that time to reflect on their own goals and objectives in life. During those times we receive much feedback from the parents on how we are doing, and hear their issues and concerns. Some parents bring up the point that they originally thought it would be terrible that they are separated from their children because they are sent to a boarding school. However, this has actually been a standard practice in many cultures for many centuries, such as in India and Europe, where children are sent off to live with other people who teach them while transmitting the educational essentials and basics of culture. Following this long proven pattern, this is what we do, too, and this age old custom does work.

In order to help our parents assist their children with the educational process, we always ask them, "What type of children do you want?" and remind them that their behavior at home must reflect what they want. For instance, one year our students had a camping trip where, because of the unpredictability of nature, we had a lot of mosquitoes and everyone got bitten. Some parents overly focused on the mosquito bites in order to try and show concern for their children, making a big fuss out of the fact. Most of the children, however, didn't care because they were used to being outdoors all the time and took this natural occurrence as a matter of course.

The question is what are you teaching your children when you focus on small inconveniences like this that will happen in life? You may think this emphasis is showing consideration, but what are you actually teaching by example? Are you helping them learn how to persevere when things aren't going perfectly well, which is a trait needed to attain your goals in life, or polluting their minds with a different type of attitude and style of thinking?

What type of children do you want them to be when they grow up? Do you want them to overly focus on and complain about small things that cannot be prevented, or do you want them to keep their eyes on the bigger picture? If you want them to achieve great things in the world, should they be taught to fixate on tiny misfortunes? What do you want to achieve as your higher outcome? This situation is just a simple example that brings up the larger issue that you must consider what you are teaching children by your words and deeds, for as a parent *you are their primary role model*. It is your behavior they will eventually copy. To a large extent, despite the many influences of their school, your children will become just like you.

This gets us back to a big question, a very big question that plagues the world today. This is the parental tendency to overprotect their children by trying to eliminate all possible risks in their lives. The world is filled with risks. Chinese culture has developed over the centuries with the uncertainties and misfortunes of life in mind, and its survival and longevity in the face of extreme difficulties is yet another reason we stress this type of thinking more than Western philosophical ideas. You, yourself, grew up with risks and your children have to learn how to manage these, too, because this is the natural way of the world. You must teach them how to live in tune with these risks.

Risks cannot be eliminated in life. Life is full of risks and you have to teach people how to live with them through mindfulness, wise decision making, and by considering the possible consequences of their actions. You certainly cannot prevent some bad things from happening in life. Therefore you must learn how to adjust yourself to deal with the ups and downs that will come with life.

If children don't learn how to do this or aren't exposed to this philosophy, they will never learn how to be strong and confident, or how to effectively and creatively deal with life challenges, problems and obstacles *as they must*. Every generation will face new obstacles which they must learn to overcome, so you must help this future generation to develop those skills in childhood rather than protect the children from everything and then throw them unprepared into the real world when they graduate from school. Everything cannot be made too easy for children in life, or they will just learn to shy away from doing the difficult but important things, or will depend on others to do everything for them. The families with nannies who do everything for the children often tell us that they see the roots of this problem in the fact that they try to be too protective or helpful.

This problem, to some extent, is now starting to hit America very hard because of an "entitlements" mentality that has replaced the ideal of self-responsibility, and we should recognize that problems like this arrive after a long period of gestation because of the poor planning of leaders and policymakers. To avoid such faults in a civilization or culture, you have to start by looking at what concepts and principles you are teaching the children, who will later be the culture bearers of that society and civilization. What you teach them when they are young is what they will adopt as their life pattern, so we feel that you should try to teach them self-reliance and being able to adaptively handle all sorts of situations so that they will be able to stand on their own two feet no matter what happens, which is what our grand teacher often emphasized. If you teach them how to think correctly from within a base of quietness, mindful, awareness and consideration, they will even make better decisions to avoid problems in the first place, which is a leadership characteristic we should all want for our countries.

You cannot just protect children from everything in life, but must expose them to the responsibility of dealing with problems and challenges. Running a boarding school, we ourselves have to expect that unexpected problems, such as accidents, will arise. Whether the children live at our school or at home, some will definitely get sick during the year because this is a natural occurrence. Some will have a toothache. Some will get into fights with other children despite our best policing – it would happen here or at another school or possibly at home as well. Some may suffer a strange accident that no one could predict or prevent just as in any ordinary school. These are ordinary, everyday life occurrences. It is impossible to 100% protect children from everything, just impossible, and parents have to accept this fact.

In modern Chinese culture this concern for *over-protection* leads to the question of raising "peach children" or "strawberry children." Society calls children who are raised with over-protection "peaches" or "strawberries" because they are so fragile that they cannot handle the real world. We get the name "strawberry" because this fruit looks so pretty on the outside, but you have to be gentle handling it since it will bruise from the slightest pressure. It cannot handle any external pressure at all. Peaches also look so firm and strong, but they also have very soft skins that bruise easily, making them difficult to transport. If you want to raise kids by avoiding all the activities that might hurt them or at which they might fail, then the danger is that they will just grow up to be like peaches and strawberries that cannot handle any pressures. They might look strong on the outside, but they are too fragile to handle big challenges, difficulties or life pressures. Children must learn how to handle risks and mistakes, and how to fail and recover from them.

Even in the West the thinking has finally changed that it is actually quite good for children to get colds or influenza when young because a bit of sickness now and then will challenge and then strengthen their immune systems. You need to go through such things to toughen up, but many parents unwisely want to remove all the risks in life for their children, and mistakenly think this is good parenting. We don't know what type of world this is preparing them to live in because it certainly is not the real one.

How can this approach properly prepare you for life? It cannot. This strategy embodies *too much love and not enough wisdom*. This is why we say you must at times let your children fail and make mistakes because the important lessons are that this can happen, and that you must spring back from this just as you must spring back from a minor burn or cut. No one can guarantee a rosy environment for their children's future, so it is far more important that they learn how to stand on their own two feet in the world rather than that they are never exposed to risks, challenges, problems or failure. Chinese culture has a long history of political upheavals, wars, famines, plagues and floods, and we are not facing our parental responsibilities if we ignore these true events and never prepare our children for being able to handle calamities. This is why we rely on Chinese philosophy, and its principles of perseverance, for teaching children how to face life.

Our school takes the attitude that everyone will face challenges in life, and you cannot just give up when you see something difficult or challenging ahead. For instance, many of our parents tell us that you cannot build a company that way but must learn how to deal with lots of problems, pressures and difficulties. If you just said to yourself that there were too many problems at the start, you would never do anything substantial at all and wouldn't get started at building or creating anything. This is not the right attitude to teach children who we all want to become creators, innovators and leaders in the next generation. Just giving them information and skills through the educational process will not help them become the guiding lights in the next generation unless we also help them to strengthen their characters and teach them perseverance in handling obstacles, so once again we must also teach them the perspective of how to handle risks and challenges.

If you look through thousands of years of Chinese history, it has been marked by countless wars, famines, droughts, floods and plagues – all sorts of catastrophes and calamities. What always helped the Chinese people survive was a concern for others that they showed by helping their families, friends and neighbors, and a cultural outlook of confidence, strength, persistence, adaptability and vigor that helped them to face and surmount these problems. We must teach children how to ignore little difficulties in life and pursue challenges with energy and vigor, rather than just give up or consistently complain about tiny difficulties.

In short, we don't believe in producing "strawberry" and "peach" children at our school. Through our outdoor programs, our camping and farming activities, and certainly though other activities as well, we hope to teach them that challenges in life are natural, and that they should ignore the bumps that happen along the way by cultivating perseverance, persistence and sometimes humility to triumph over them.

We always tell the parents that they must be role models for educating the children just as we try to make our teachers role models too. The educational burden is not just on the school, but on the parents. When a parent says, "My kid hates English," We ask, "Do you like English?" When we hear them say that they also hate English, we have to warn them that they might be passing this attitude onto their children in some way, and if so this is affecting their learning. We actually find that the children who have the most trouble learning English also have parents who have this attitude, and somehow it gets passed along to the children to affect their learning process in a negative way.

The education of children in so many areas is therefore a joint parent-school responsibility. Both sides have to be careful about what they do and say. The school cannot assume the educational burden all on its own without parental support and as previously stated, the absolutely best results come when the parents clearly support the school and its efforts. Then the messages being transmitted to the children will run deep and consistently, and the children will absorb those influences.

As parents, you must also provide a humanistic role model and learning role model for your children. For instance, if you want children to be honest then you have to be honest yourself, and they must see this in action. You have to become a model of personal integrity if you also want to have virtuous children because they will certainly mimic your behavior. If you want your children to study better, then when they come home and do their homework, instead of promising them a reward for finishing their homework, you might read a book while they are working and let them see that you are also reading. When they see you reading or studying, then from your example they pick up the idea that this process is important. In this way they will naturally absorb the idea that education is important because they will say to themselves, "Even my parents are doing it, so this must really be the way things should be done. It is not just the school that is valuing this." The whole family should value education and the love of learning, and you must learn how to carry forward various educational ideas into your family. Then the children will do well with whatever they later choose to study and master as their career and calling in life.

Parents also often forget that they are parents and can set different rules for their children that don't apply to themselves. Moms and dads can have their own rules for living that are different from children's rules. Some mothers, for instance, say that since they watch TV then in fairness they should let their children watch television for the same amount of time. Well, that's not true. You can set up whatever rules you want within your household for the children because parents are parents and children are children. The rules can be different because everyone has different roles they must play. You just have to be careful of the results that your rules are producing and *be careful not to have too many*, which is unwise. The more rules you have, the unhappier your children will be due to the restraints, and the harder it will be to enforce them all.

Many parents today are overly lenient or spoil their children by not setting any home rules because they don't want to see their children cry or whine, and they want to be seen as their child's friend rather than as the "bad guy." They don't realize that children who get into trouble the most easily often have overly permissive parents who don't set any standards, and the kids *take this lack of rules as a sign that their parents don't care*, even though the parents think it shows that they are totally loving and accepting.

To help parents out, we want them to know that much research shows it is the parents who set rules they *enforce consistently*, but who find a way to *be flexible so that the rule setting process is respected,* who have the most honest children who lie the least, which is the characteristic parents most often say they want in their children. The parents with the best relationships with their children set some rules over just a few key spheres of influence and then expect their child to obey those rules. In other areas they allow their children to make their own decisions.

Most parents think that the opposite of honesty is lying, but in children's minds the opposite of lying is actually *arguing.* When a child is arguing with you he is trying to be honest. To say it another way, in children's minds the opposite of arguing is not compromise but lying. If a child didn't argue with you then a typical strategy is to pretend to go along with your wishes and then secretly do what they want anyway. Children argue with you because they want to be honest! Hence, when children argue with you that the rules you set are too restrictive, despite the uncomfortable situation, the fact that they argue with you is because they are actually *being honest and want to abide by rules.* They are not challenging your authority to set rules but simply want them to be different.

Parents rarely realize, because of the uncomfortable stresses of those challenging situations, that arguing is not necessarily being disrespectful. The children have an inner integrity that they are trying to respect rather than simply agreeing with you and then breaking those rules in secret. As a parent, you must understand this aspect of human nature and change your ways accordingly.

The idea of parents being parents and children being children brings up yet another problem in parenting today. This is an issue that has much greater importance with older children in their teens, and even though we do not deal for teenage children who are facing these issues, it is still important to bring up this topic, often mentioned by Nan Huai-chin. This is the fact that many parents believe that they know what is best for their children, and therefore go too far in this direction by overriding all of their children's personal desires and preferences. We often don't let them pursue interests that we don't agree with, but which are perfectly harmless.

This is unfortunate because you certainly cannot predict whether your child will grow up to be a writer, dancer, pilot, doctor, official or businessman when they show early signs of any special interests. You absolutely cannot predict their final career or occupation in life, and sometimes they need to pursue unusual interests in order to grow. Because of their past life tendencies, they each have their own dreams rather than our dreams for their lives. Therefore we shouldn't try to subconsciously force children down a path we have decided they should take to fulfill our own ambitions just as we should not immediately stomp on any of their dreams and interests or tell them that they cannot become something later on in life.

As long as they hold to virtuous aspirations, we should let them sing the melody they have in their own heads because the world is waiting for them to hammer it into the shape they want that can far exceed anyone's expectations. Sometimes a road they wish to take may seem foolish, yet often that road of personal interest leads to a greatness which no one could have predicted. You should certainly give young adults the benefits of your wisdom by dispensing advice, but let them pursue their interests and love what they do and do what they love while recognizing that they must make their own mistakes as part of the learning process.

The ideas of career-based education in early childhood, or any type of predictive testing, is very questionable. We feel you should primarily focus on helping children establish a good values-based foundation for life so that they become good people, and teach them the skills they need to survive as they slowly carve out their own life direction. Who can guess what that final direction will be? Even in college students sometimes change their majors several times.

As our grand teacher Nan Huai-chin once wrote, "From time immemorial to the present, parents may, unconsciously, want their children to fulfill things they couldn't personally do in their entire lives, regardless of their children's real interests and inborn character. This seems to be the same in all countries and yet it is the most typical fault one could make with education. What we need to do as parents is think about how to cultivate our children in a correct way so that they grow up to be virtuous and independent. If all that parents see in their children is a future reached by going to school and succeeding in taking examinations, I can tell you it is a huge mistake. Their love will bring their children real harm rather than any real benefits."

For very young children this problem is not as severe because parents are so busy with all the tasks involved in just raising them, but as they enter into their later teen and college years, parents often sometimes try to live out their own unrealized dreams through the lives of their children. With their own unrealized dreams in mind, they sometimes try to push their children down particular paths that are totally unsuited to them, which is then a grave mistake and also a complete failure of parental responsibility.

The result of this coercion is usually totally different from what parents had hoped for because the young adults feel thwarted in pursuing their own dreams of happiness. They don't always need to restrict their studies to topics that are "more useful" in having a utility for work, and if they are forced to follow a career path for which they have no interest, how can they truly find happiness in life, which is what we actually want them to experience?

Do we want our children to be miserable or happy in life? Do we want them to live a comfortable, prosperous adult life while *dead inside* because they have become a slave to the requirements of living according to some socially accepted "respectable role"? Is the extra income we want our children to have worth them being miserable in life doing something for a living that they don't like doing? You must consider the terrible waste of time, money and energy when many young adults who enroll in study programs to become doctors or lawyers then drop out, or graduate and then never practice, because they discover they were pushed into pursuing career paths their parents favored but which did not truly appeal to their own hearts.

If we coerce our children into career paths that promise large pay checks, while ignoring their inner hearts, can we say that they are then truly living a life of success? A large pay check is simply a monetary result, and who knows what emotional sufferings stand behind it? Isn't success in life better represented by a child earning less income but who is making his own way in life in a field he loves, who is very happy, and who has a supporting, loving family?

You should want your children to find their own independent calling in life that accords with their innermost interests because that is when they will be happiest, regardless of the eventual degree of wealth, status, power or fame

They achieve. You should want your children to grow up being virtuous people who live an honest and ethical life committed to moral principles, and who are likely to do the right thing even under difficult circumstances, rather than attain riches from corruption, such as having cheated others for money. You want them to develop *a sense of responsibility that is greater than a sense of entitlement* which predisposes them to unethical actions. No one wants children who grow up hurting others and society while covering up their infractions with all sorts of excuses. Many desire status, fame, power and wealth but it is impossible for everyone to succeed, just as all of us cannot be "number one" for some attribute. Such standings are always fleeting anyway. Wealth and power are not things that can last, and we should not measure human values or the value of human lives according to such materialistic notions.

Without intending to do so, parents forcing children down a career path they dislike often plant the seeds of a rebellious psychology that will lead a young adult into rejecting both the family and community because of their dissatisfaction. The ties within the family will then be damaged and society will suffer the needless loss of human talent. Parents need to focus on just giving their children a good foundation and helping them cultivate their basic skills and character. Later they will find their own paths to success. They need to learn to relax about such matters and let their children find their own way to reach their true potential.

Building a virtuous character, and establishing this result as the foundation of happiness and success, is therefore one of the most important things in education. It is the key to everything we have been discussing rather than the fact one can force a child into a career that we think will bring them fortune, fame and *our* happiness rather than *their* happiness. We all want our children to grow up in life being happy and successful, but in our deepest minds we somehow mistakenly feel that this ties in with becoming rich. Even if that were truly the case, no one can predict how your children will make money when they grow up, and if that is the case, you must ask yourself what is the best way to educate them in the face of such uncertainty? What is the absolute best foundation to give them?

That foundation should be practical, but it should also reflect spiritual content. It should incorporate the fact that the child has become a good human being. It should reflect the best of the East and West and combine natural science with philosophy, practical materialism and spirituality. It should include giving children the skills for navigating through life and stress virtue, wisdom and the fact that there are short term and long-term consequences to actions.

As Nan Huai-chin said, it is impossible for every child to have the fate of becoming rich. Making money is one of the necessities of life, but should *not be the target of life*. Carrying out your life purpose should be the target of your life. On the other hand, we can certainly help our children develop character traits that will help them secure a good living and be happy at whatever calling or level of success which fate brings. Therefore we take the stand of educating children by primarily stressing good personality traits and the skills necessary for living, and in this way help them establish a strong foundation in their elementary years that will help them become happy and successful in life.

Once again, we are not focused on grades at our school, but on teaching virtue and life skills. Even companies have started to find out that grades, SAT scores, or even the prestige of which school you went to have nothing to do with your job performance. Your career performance, or success in life, has much to do with the factors we normally call working habits, character traits, personality factors, and your value system or thinking process, which is why we emphasize these things rather than just academic skill sets to be mastered. Even though we don't make grades and IQ our target, our method actually produces children who often outperform others along academic lines when their skills are measured, and perhaps it is a result of the way we teach them. Grades are not our focus because our objective is more along the lines of Confucius, who said, "I broaden myself with culture and restrain myself with proper standards of behavior." However, we certainly are not perfect so we are constantly examining our own shortcomings and developing new methods and strategies as we try to create a new Chinese educational model.

We want to conclude this discussion with a quote from Warren Buffett, one of the richest men in the world who is often admired for his wisdom. Perhaps you will not believe us about the importance of the human qualities of character and virtue, but will instead believe the billionaire Warren Buffet because of his elevated standing. Buffett once made a speech to college graduates that confirmed what we are taking as the emphasis of our educational model. Warren Buffett said,

> What if you could buy 10% of one of your classmates and their future earnings? You wouldn't buy the ones with the highest IQ, the best grades, etc., but the most effective. You like people who are generous, go out of their way, straight shooters. Now imagine that you could short 10% of one of your classmates. This part is usually more fun as you start looking around the room. You wouldn't choose the ones with the poorest grades. Look for people nobody wants to be around, that are obnoxious or like to take all the credit. If you have a 500 HP engine and only get 50 HP out of it, you'll be beat by someone else that has a 300 HP engine but gets 250 HP output. The difference between potential and output comes from human qualities. You can make a list of the qualities you admire and those you despise. To turn the tables, think if this is the way I react to the qualities on the list, which is the way the world will react to me. You can learn to turn on those qualities you want and turn off those qualities you wish to avoid. The chains of habit are too light to be felt until they are too heavy to be broken. You can't change at 60; the time to look at that list is now.

As educators and parents, we are entrusted not just with our own futures but the future of our society and nation through our children, who are our posterity, so the educational emphasis of our school is to lay the foundation that simply helps children become good people. How can we expect these future leaders of society to guide us on the right track if their own sense of direction, of what is right and wrong, is dulled because of a lack of virtue?

We therefore try to help them establish a foundation of deep culture, wisdom and virtue in their lives. We also want to introduce them to a *broad cultural content* that will enrich their lives in many ways, and which they can draw on throughout their years. We want to give them a familiarity with the right methods so that they can cultivate themselves along spiritual pathways later in life, if they wish, and accomplish the goals of *The Great Learning* that are also the goals of Taoism, Buddhism and many other Chinese philosophical schools. This is a goal to harmonize the practical concerns of life with spirituality.

The future careers of our children, or the things they will accomplish in life as well as the ultimate heights to which they will eventually rise, are not something anyone can predict. However, we can certainly say that their destiny will depend on their personalities, values, and the correct or incorrect use of their minds since their thoughts become their behaviors. Furthermore, wisdom should be something a person can cultivate and then call on for any situation that arises, so we stress *both virtue and wisdom* in our educational process. The merit of having wealth, fame or high status in life is fleeting, whereas we want the virtue of each child to become something dependable that others can rely upon as a constant.

While we teach many things, as we have tried to briefly introduce, our school is particularly devoted to this simple idea of emphasizing a virtuous spiritual or moral life, self-responsibility, and the wisdom of Chinese culture in how to live, deal with things, and make decisions. As stated, the "operating system" we wish to install in children's lives is based on the best of Chinese culture and philosophy, and the "software" we teach includes the best from all over the world just as you would find in any international school. By teaching life skills, we help the children develop a sense of independence, self-reliance, self-esteem, empowerment and achievement that cannot be achieved by other means. By emphasizing integrity and respect, we help children cultivate mindfulness and awareness as well as kindness, sincerity and appreciation. This is also one of the many ways we help children develop their powers of concentration. We also teach the children various means by which they can adjust their bodies and minds, and provide them with a secular foundation and familiarity with self-cultivation so that they can pursue this later in life if they choose to do so. We teach them how to become able to direct their own lives, create and learn new things on their own, and do better things for themselves and the world. We focus on transmitting to them the meaning of the Chinese classics, and the best methods, influences and philosophies of Western civilization, so they can find their own meaning and purpose for life. We are committed to creating an authentic learning environment that doesn't just teach academically, but leads to true personal growth in everyone who is involved.

While we talked primarily of Chinese culture, we try to provide a unifying basis of the best of Western and Chinese cultural thought for the next generation—what is truthful and works well, anchored in wisdom and virtue, rather than something superficial or superstitious—and we hope it thereby creates the next generation of leaders who will help the world, helps children to cultivate and develop themselves properly so that they can contribute to society, and does its own little bit in helping to thwart the degeneration of civilization.

It is often a daunting challenge to take on this task, but we find that following the indications of our grand teacher, Nan Huai-chin, along the lines of what is the best development road for humanity, and putting his philosophies into effect has often given us energy when we realize that we are devoted to a larger mission of helping the future generations live a better life than the present. This is what we all hope for the future of China, and for the other countries that wish to bring culture and values back into their educational systems.

CONTACT INFORMATION

If as an organization or educator you are interested in joining with us to assist in our goal of creating a new model of Chinese schooling that incorporates the best of both Chinese and Western culture and civilization, or if you are interested in teaching at our school or attending our one-year Teacher's Certification Program, please feel free to contact us at:

Sami Kuo, Principal and Founder
Wujiang Taihu International School
No. 8 Yanhu Dong Road
Miaogang District, Qidu Town
Wujiang City, Jiangsu Province, China 215232
sami88@yeah.net

TaihuSchool.com

www.ingramcontent.com/pod-product-compliance
Lightning Source LLC
Chambersburg PA
CBHW052010090426
42741CB00008B/1633

* 9 780615 824727 *